Improvising Shakespeare
Reading for the Stage

Improvising Shakespeare

Reading for the Stage

Thomas S. Turgeon
Kenyon College

The McGraw-Hill Companies, Inc.

New York St. Louis San Francisco Auckland Bogotá Caracas
Lisbon London Madrid Mexico City Milan Montreal New Delhi
Paris San Juan Singapore Sydney Tokyo Toronto

McGraw-Hill

A Division of The McGraw-Hill Companies

IMPROVISING SHAKESPEARE
Reading for the Stage

This book is printed on acid-free paper.

1 2 3 4 5 6 7 8 9 0 (FGR FGR) 9 0 9 8 7 6

ISBN 0-07-065522-7

This book was set in Palatino by ComCom, Inc.
The editor was Cynthia Ward; the editing manager was Peggy Rehberger;
the cover was designed by Lisa Cicchetti; cover photo by Arthur Tres/Photonica;
the production supervisor was Richard A. Ausburn.
Project supervision was by Spectrum Publisher Services, Inc.
Quebecor Printing/Fairfield was printer and binder.

Library of Congress Cataloging-in-Publication Data
Turgeon, Thomas S.
    Improvising Shakespeare:reading for the stage / Thomas S. Turgeon.
        p.   cm.
    Includes bibliographical references (p.   ) and index.
    ISBN 0-07-065522-7 (acid-free paper)
    1. Shakespeare, William, 1564-1616—Dramatic production.
2. Improvisation (Acting)   3. Oral interpretation.   4. Oral reading.
5. Acting.   I. Title.
PR3091.T87   1996
792' .028—dc20   96-27273

http://www.mhcollege.com

About the Author

THOMAS S. TURGEON is Professor and Chair of the Department of Dance and Drama at Kenyon College, Gambier, Ohio. After graduation from Amherst College and election to Phi Beta Kappa, he received his Doctor of Fine Arts degree in Directing from the Yale School of Drama, studying as a Woodrow Wilson Fellow. In 27 years of teaching and working in the professional theater, he has directed more than 45 productions, acted several classical and modern roles, and translated and/or adapted 16 texts from the French and Greek classics for the stage.

For
Peggy, Sarah, and Charles

Contents

Preface

For 27 years, I have been teaching college actors, directors, and many others who are trying to learn how to bring dramatic texts to the stage. Most of them begin their work presuming that they are supposed to read plays (particularly the plays of Shakespeare) as subjects for historical, cultural, anthropological, political, or aesthetic debate. Throughout their academic lives, they've heard and accepted the argument that plays are meant to be elaborate instruments of advocacy.

So when students with this sort of preparation in dramatic literature come to study theatre, they tend to arrive ready to discuss issues, argue about themes, and analyze imagery. But very few of them, for all their enthusiasm and curiosity about the stage, are equipped to imagine fresh performances as they read. They can recognize an allusion in a minute, but they don't know how to participate in the creation of a new illusion.

It comes as a surprise to many of them to discover that the first step is to learn that the theatre demands that they master a different kind of reading. In the process of rehearsal, actors and directors must learn to explore these famous texts as scripts rather than as artifacts or as manifestos. That is, in the theatre, the playwright's work becomes part of an active and pragmatic collaboration. It's this collaboration that can, in the end, produce a new and original illusion for the stage.

Improvising Shakespeare is designed to help these students begin. It's premise is that there are two distinct ways of reading a dramatic text: There is the familiar kind of interpretation that typically goes on in a classroom—a noble pursuit of literary study that reveals many things, but an academic approach that working theatre people tend to find distracting and irrelevant to the practical job at hand. There is also the kind of reading and study that actually goes on in a rehearsal hall—an equally rigorous and exacting approach to the text that nobody talks about much in campus settings. This is the process of analysis used by actors, directors, and all the other collaborators whose imagining and labor complete the play implicit in the words on the page.

The purpose of this book is to introduce, and to put into practice, this second kind of reading.

A word about the title: *Improvising Shakespeare* might seem to be an invitation to self-indulgence, to an "anything goes" approach to the texts, which suggests that if the words on the page give students any trouble, they needn't worry; they have only to make up new words they find more convenient. Not so. In the kind of reading described here, the playwright's words and the structure of his plot are presumed inviolable.

But the theatrical illusion does not exist in a book; long after the words and the structure of the action are set in type, there remains an astonishing number of decisions and inventions to be made before we can realize a complete illusion for the stage from a received text. The title *Improvising Shakespeare* (derived from an apposite remark from English director Jonathan Miller) is intended to suggest the process of energetic discovery it takes to make all the choices left to a company of actors as they read, explore, and rehearse.

There are, of course, fundamental understandings, rules of the game for this kind of work. These axioms are laid out in the Introduction. Chapters 1–3 make the theoretical arguments that define this alternative sort of reading and demonstrate that the theatrical method of exploring the text I am describing is an extension of the nature of theatre as an art form.

The rest of the book puts this theory into practice. Chapter 4 describes what to look for as you read to imagine theatrically useful ideas. Then Chapters 5–11 each examine the theatrical implications of one of these steps in the reading process by exploring a famous scene from Shakespeare as if we were talking it over in rehearsal.

These chapters are meant to be "interactive." That is, they ask students to stretch their imaginations by developing their own theatrical understandings of the incidents indicated on the page. The process is taken from my own teaching; I lay out the text and then ask questions, lots of them. As illustration and guidance along the way, I include examples of solutions to the problems I pose, which actors and directors who have spent their careers performing classical texts have tried. But in the end, students will learn the best way to participate when they find answers on their own. The "improvisations," the imaginative answers to the mysteries and opportunities posed by a close theatrical reading of the text, are left to them.

One hope behind this book is that students who picture themselves working in the theatre will learn a new way to use their imaginations as they read dramatic texts. Another hope is that students of literature, or anyone who simply loves these plays, will catch a glimpse of what stimulating and evocative surprises can emerge once the theatrical imagination is put to work.

Thomas S. Turgeon

Introduction

To begin with, this is not a book about Shakespeare. It's a book about reading; reading and imagining for the theatre.

If you went to a rehearsal hall where a company of trained and experienced actors was working to produce one of Shakespeare's plays, in one end of the hall you might see some of the cast working on a section of the play with the director; they could be going over a moment, adjusting a bit of stage business, speculating together about the reason for a gesture, or trying out a new sound or rhythm for a speech. To the side, you would be apt to find others waiting their turn, watching, chatting quietly, writing a letter, or listening to a Walkman. But if you were to look around the back of the room, you would find other actors, alone and hard at work. Perched on a windowsill or on an unused platform, the actors are reading the text of the play. Long after many choices for their eventual performances have been made and rehearsed, even after they have broken the back of the memorization problem and (almost) know their lines, they are still reading their scripts. They are reading and noticing, reading and making associations, reading and remembering, reading and imagining. Experienced actors read, re-read, and re-read again.

There are, of course, a lot of reasons for reading a dramatic text, particularly one written by William Shakespeare. Readers look to these texts for cultural enrichment, philosophical insight, passionate advocacy, or lyric beauty, and they find these wonders in profusion.

Actors find these things as well, of course, but actors also have a unique job ahead of them. When an actor's work is done, there will be a new Portia, a new Hamlet, a new Thersites, or a new Queen Margaret. Although beautiful abstractions and stimulating commentary can be as engaging to an actor as to anybody else, they also can be distracting and irrelevant to the job at hand. No abstractions, no matter how interesting, are "actions that a man might play." When all the commentary is done, Shakespeare's famous words are still waiting on the page to be informed by the actor as they never have been informed before.

Reading to imagine a new way to inform the text is a unique process. It is a test for the imagination that is fundamental and peculiar to the working theatre. For our purposes, Shakespeare was, first and foremost, a man of the theatre; he wrote so that his words would be informed by his collaborators at the Globe. Since then, his playscripts have continued to invite actors, directors, designers, and musicians on invigorating journeys of the imagination.

Peter Brook describes this journey of invention that he himself has taken so often and with such success:

> Shakespeare had the largest vocabulary of any English poet, constantly adding to the words at his disposal, combining obscure philosophical terms with the crudest of obscenities, until eventually there were over 25,000 at his fingertips. In the theatre, there are infinitely more languages, beyond words, through which communication is established and maintained with the audience. There is body language, sound language, rhythm language, color language, costume language, scenery language, lighting language—all to be added to those 25,000 words.[1]

Most readers of Shakespeare claim that they are discovering what is in the text. Brook suggests another kind of reading altogether, one where the job is to imagine what is *not* in the text, but what will, in a process of discovery and invention, emerge from the act of reading that text to complete a play implicit in it.

The actors around the walls of our imaginary rehearsal hall are right in the middle of their odyssey. This book is about learning to join them.

A few axioms for this work:

1. Unfortunately, too many people think of Shakespeare's plays as things printed in books and assigned for high school and college classes. Our work requires another way of thinking about plays. When I use the word "play," I mean the completed piece of theatrical art, the whole play, the imagined and designed public occasion where a story is enacted before a watching and listening audience.

2. Shakespeare's texts (or any playwright's texts) initiate and shape the process of making a play. But our work requires that we understand that they are scripts, things that by their very nature are incomplete. It is the actor's assignment, along with the director, designers, musicians, and all the rest of the company of collaborators who inhabit a theatre, to finish the job, to *complete* the play.

3. The actor Philip Franks remembers rehearsing *Hamlet* under the direction of Roger Michell at the Royal Shakespeare Company:

> When I first met Roger to discuss the play we both found that large questions of definition or interpretation were not of much use. We skirted around the usual ones—what is the play saying? Who is Hamlet? Is his madness real or feigned?—and discarded them, with relief, in favor of a detailed and organic approach, a mining of the text and discussion of particular relationships. Thereafter, we hardly ever talked about 'interpretation', only about the choices available within a scene, a speech, a line or a word.[2]

As Philip Franks suggests, one useful thing to do in this context is lay aside the word "interpretation," at least in its commonly understood sense. An actor needs to know that a play requires no commentary to become complete in the imagination of an audience. "Completing the play" does not mean using the theatre to illustrate the historical assertions or literary criticism or partisan advocacy produced by other kinds of reading. Rather, it means making specific choices in order to complete a self-sustaining enactment of a story capable of engaging the imagination of the audience. A play needs to be an occasion complete in and of itself.

4. Here, again, is Peter Brook:

> The theatre is in no way a discussion between cultivated people. The theatre, through the energy of sound, word, colour, and movement, touches an emotional button that in turn sends tremors through the intellect.[3]

It is this process of perception in the theatre that other kinds of reading tend to skip. Cultivated discussion is apt to jump directly from text to interpretation, leaving out a spectator's physical and emotional experience of the occasion in the theatre. In our work, however, intellectual tremors and scholarly interpretation can be eventual *results* of the experience in the theatre, but are no substitutes for it; the emotional impact of the completed play comes first.

5. Plays, no matter how important they have become, are exercises in make-believe. They are always, in a sense, "play" (and this is part of their delight). They offer their stories through elaborately artificial events. So, if this theatrical experience is going to have a chance

of moving an audience, of touching those "emotional buttons," it has to persuade a theatre full of intelligent and sensible people to go along with what is, after all, an obvious sham.

6. Since a play cannot persuade an audience of its authority by being "real life," a play must persuade by being coherent. It is the creation of a persuasive coherence on the stage that makes the towering fictions, the magic and fantasy, the pageantry, and the distilled intensity of Shakespeare's action convincing.

7. Therefore, every element of the performance, those elements in the text and those yet to be imagined, must be coherent and connected by a recognizable logic. Everything the audience witnesses on the stage must appear to have a reason *from within the play itself* for happening when and how it happens. Every choice each artist makes must appear to be a seamless extension of every other choice made by everyone else working on the play—including the very specific choices made by the playwright and recorded in the text.

8. Reading to imagine a new way to inform Shakespeare's words, then, means reading to imagine a new and persuasive coherence for the completed play that the audience will eventually see. Thus, learning to read for the stage means learning to ask the sort of questions that can lead you to imagine such a coherence.

A bit of warning first—as you might expect from the previous axioms, there are many sorts of questions and answers about these texts that do *not* help the actor much. Among the most common, perhaps, are these: "Yes, but what is Shakespeare trying to *say?*" and, "I don't get it; what can I do to it to make it relevant?"

The reason these questions distract the actor is that they lead a reader's thinking away from the play he or she is working to complete. Answers to the first question tend to sound like this: "*King Lear?* It's Shakespeare's *Dies Irae*, his song of mourning for a lost world"; "*Hamlet* dramatizes the conflicts of a society in fundamental cultural transition"; "In *The Taming of the Shrew*, we can see Shakespeare's proto-feminist sympathies"; and so on. At best, the text serves as a subject for a rewarding discussion; at worst, the work is reduced to a slogan of assigned significance. In neither case do we end up with a play.

Answers to the second question are no more promising: "What if we dressed Julius Caesar as The Godfather?"; "I heard that somebody in Canada put the opposing armies of *Henry V* in the 'armor' of opposing hockey teams, one French, one English . . . "; or "Wouldn't Macbeth be more relevant if he were a Native American?" Particular productions that have set these famous stories in unexpected places and times have been wonderful. However, as a general proposition, the relevancy argument—the sensed need to make these plays into topically "significant" occasions—tends to lead to interpretive "concepts" that displace the play rather than complete it.

How do we learn the right sort of questions to ask? How do we recognize the most promising answers?

The first part of this book attempts to define an actor's kind of reading in theoretical terms. The principle at work here is that certain kinds of questions and answers—certain kinds of reading—are organic extensions of the fundamental nature of the theatre itself. A clear and specific understanding of the job at hand can go a long way toward sorting out the most productive approaches to a text.

In the second part, we try out the principle. This is going to take some active participation on your part. We take some of Shakespeare's most familiar scenes and explore them as an actor or a director might, asking their sort of questions as we go through the text line by line. Although there are a lot of questions, they are only examples. It is hoped that with practice you will soon have questions of your own.

In any case, I'm leaving all the answers to you. Don't skim over these questions, but take your time. Don't leave a question until you have invented and chosen an answer that plausibly fits the text and also engages your imagination.

As you accumulate your choices, you'll be learning to invent, to improvise your own coherence for everything you see on the page. You'll find that you always need to be specific in your answers, utterly faithful to the words you've been given, literal, concrete, and logical. You'll also learn how stimulating your choices can be when they become surprising, colorful, unexpected, funny, or dangerous. In short, you'll do what our rehearsing actors are doing; reading to imagine, re-reading to inform, and continuing to read to the point of improvising Shakespeare.

PART ONE

Theory

CHAPTER 1

Two Kinds of Reading

Shakespeare is essentially a dramatist, and drama is not, in the strict sense, "literature."[4]

—SUZANNE LANGER

It's safe to say that no one who has set words on paper so that they might be spoken by actors has stimulated more reading than William Shakespeare. This despite the wishes of the playwright, who, history tells us, spent a good deal of energy trying to keep his writings for the stage out of the hands of printers and publishers of books. To make a living, Shakespeare needed to get people to set down their coins at the theatre door, paying good money for the opportunity to see his plays and hear his words, not read them.

Fortunately, Shakespeare failed to keep his plays out of print. He would probably be surprised to learn that reading a Shakespearean text has become a far more common experience than seeing one performed in a theatre.

It's a generality of course, and exceptions can be found, but as a rule most approaches to reading these texts tend to fall into two categories, the one, typical of a classroom, and the other, part of the work that goes on in a rehearsal hall.

Consider, for example, these two published summaries of the same moment in *Hamlet*, the incident of the Player King's great speech:

This episode is intrinsically entertaining, as well as highly suggestive of the playwright's attitude toward his profession and toward the actual theatrical situation in 1599–1601 when there was a war of satires among the theatres. In a measure Shakespeare has made Hamlet his own spokesman in deprecating the slurs cast upon the *common players* (338–44) such as himself. Polonius continues to exhibit his folly and Hamlet his intellectual agility and human many-sidedness. Observe his kindness to the players, his sudden reference to universal sinfulness (515–17), and his concern lest others follow his example in mocking Polonius (529). At one point the vogue of the child actors is unexpectedly equated by Hamlet with the popularity of the new King Claudius (355–59) whose *picture in little* commands such high prices . . . Hamlet's allusion to Polonius as *Jephtha* (393–408) is significant, in view of the fact that Jephtha sacrificed a beloved daughter and that Ophelia is, however unwittingly, sacrificed by her father. The Player's speech provides occasion for a display of histrionic passion which Hamlet will later remark upon, but its length is much greater than this simple function necessitates and one suspects the presence of an element of parody in the stiff rhetoric and bombastic metaphor. However distended the treatment, this episode serves the purpose of showing the inception of Hamlet's device in trapping his uncle with the play-within-the-play.[5]

Compare this review of the scene with another:

At today's rehearsal . . . George Voscovec was at last given an opportunity to practice his important and exacting speech as the Player King . . . Few theatregoers understand the crucial nature of this monologue, since, on the surface, it seems no more than a set-piece: a golden opportunity for an old school actor to show off his resonant technique. On the contrary, the actual purpose of the Player King's speech is all but seminal. It stimulates in Hamlet the notion "to have these players play something like the murder of my father before mine uncle." In other words, the Player King teases to the surface Hamlet's quite probably latent impulse to rewrite *The Murder of Gonzago* as a mousetrap for Claudius . . .

To begin with, it is of value for the Player King to suggest to the audience (emotionally) that he is an *actor acting* . . . but, on no account must the actor evade the most touching truth of all: ham or no ham, the Player King genuinely "forced his soul to his own conceit." He is genuinely moved, genuinely distracted, genuinely tearful . . .

Hamlet regards the Player King's control of his soul as "monstrous." Indeed it is. And precisely because it *is* so monstrous, proceeding as it does from a mere fiction, a dream of passion, Hamlet is galvanized into action. After the self-berating of the "O, what a rogue and peasant slave am I" soliloquy, he never really retreats from his purpose again.[6]

Alfred Harbage, who recorded the first summary of the scene, was, at the time, Cabot Professor of English at Harvard. The second response to the text was in a published series of letters the actor William Redfield wrote to a friend while he was rehearsing to play Guildenstern in the Richard Burton/John Gielgud production.

These two readers, both giving the same pages of text an imaginative and informed examination, might be talking about different scenes. The purposes they propose, the techniques they find, and the aesthetic riches they celebrate as they record their understanding of the text seem almost unrelated by the language they are reading in common.

The question is not which one of them is "right" and which is "wrong." The question for our purposes here is which way of thinking about a text is more useful for the stage, and, more important, why.

In his piece, what Professor Harbage advises his readers to look for is the references he sees Shakespeare making to the actual history of the Elizabethan theatre. He points out how Shakespeare uses the words of this scene to comment on his own theatrical experience, on the competition he faced from Henry Evan's company of child actors playing to success in Blackfriars in the 1599–1600 season, and to the supposed tendency of rival Edward Alleyn and his fellow actors at the Rose to act bombastically whenever they got a chance to tear into a thrilling speech ("... there was a war of satires among the theatres."). For Harbage, the meaning and the delight of the scene is to be found in extracting from its virtuoso performance a view of the real world articulated by the playwright.

In order to express this view to the critically minded reader, Harbage assumes that Shakespeare's primary task, as an artist, was manipulating the words he was arranging for the characters to speak. Every proposal Harbage suggests for the meaning of the scene is carefully supported by a citation of a particular word or phrase: "At one point the vogue of the child actors is unexpectedly equated by

Hamlet with the popularity of the new King Claudius (355–59) whose *picture in little* commands such high prices," he writes. Shakespeare's choice of a word, image, simile, or metaphor is to be understood in the end as the playwright's effort to describe or comment on his own rich view of human experience, those phenomena he has observed in the actual world, the world outside of, but represented by, the language of the play.

In this approach to the text, the medium of the art of playwriting is presumed to be language. A playwright is thought of as a writer, an artist in the same general category as the novelist, the poet, and the short story writer. Plays are, of course, distinct from novels and verse because they are written for the stage, a difference Harbage acknowledges in detail.[7] Still, once they are stripped of theatrical decoration and convention, plays are understood to be essentially the same as other forms of art that achieve their impact through the manipulation of language. In the classroom, typically, drama is read as if it were a genre of literature.

Working from these, or analogous, assumptions, other literary readers have proposed all sorts of interpretations of Shakespeare's texts. There seems to be an infinite number of "Shakespeares" to listen to and learn from, many of them far more specialized, argumentative, abstract, political, accusatory, or apocalyptic than the Shakespeare suggested by Harbage's gentle evocation of the world of the Elizabethan stage. Over the years schools of criticism proliferate, each reacting to, and often rejecting, those that have gone before. Critical theories about Shakespeare's true intentions rise and claim the field, stand or fall, fade away, or rise to fight again.

One reason for this can be found in an observation offered by poet and Shakespearean scholar Frederick Turner. In his book *Natural Classicism*, he observes that most literary criticism of the plays of Shakespeare is "kalogenic" in nature; that is, it is an act of interpretation in which the object of the reading is to assign a particular ethical value to the work of art.[8] The meaning of a word, a speech, a gesture, an act, or the text as a whole is to be found in the judgment it appears to express, the values it seems to endorse as it illustrates a particular view of the human condition.

It follows that the reason most literary readers find and write about so many "Shakespeares" is that so many distinct values, so many expressions of opinion and judgment, can be found through the literary explication of the texts for these complex plays. Happily, there is no end to the values readers find strengthened by these dramatic poems.

Still, the aesthetic assumptions of these analyses tend to remain constant regardless of the particular cases readers seek to make. Shakespeare is a writer—the text for one of his plays should be read as a complete and self-sufficient masterwork of literature, a profoundly expressive art object that is constructed out of language. To read these texts in this way is to analyze the language chosen by the author, to recognize the ways that language was shaped, to speculate about those forces and values in the actual world that impelled the author to form his language as he did, and to respond analytically to those brilliant constructions of linguistic art.

To use Aristotle's word, the object of literary reading is to find, and make a persuasive case for, an *ethos* for the work.

Conclusions of the sort Professor Harbage draws often seem beside the point to actors and directors. John Barton, in the Preface to *Playing Shakespeare*, notes:

> For many years I have heard actors lament that they could find nothing written which would assist them directly in handling his (Shakespeare's) text and particularly his verse. Although there is no lack of material about all aspects of his plays and stagecraft, most actors feel that this does not really help them as actors.[9]

Actors' frustration with the bulk of literary explanations of Shakespearean texts is not because these conclusions are too "difficult" or obscure. It is simply because most of them tend to be arguments based on presumptions about drama that the actor, working from practical experience, finds inapplicable to his or her work.

Unlike Harbage's summary, the letter from William Redfield barely mentions the actual world Shakespeare might have known. Shakespeare may well have had opinions about his theatrical competitors as he composed the Pyrrhus speech for his Player King to speak, but Redfield knows that no actor can enact a reference, a world view, or a "value." What an actor needs is action. So, at this point, Redfield's attention is focused on a moment-to-moment understanding of what's going on *within* the scene, the fictional world of Hamlet and the Player King in action.

As he reads within the confines of the scene, he finds the spectacle of the Player weeping as he performs his bombast "all but seminal" (as opposed to "intrinsically entertaining"). Redfield finds the scene profoundly important to the play as a whole, whereas Harbage describes the scene as Shakespeare's "distended" observations about interesting but secondary issues.

This is more than simply a difference of opinion or taste between two readers. Rather, it suggests that for Redfield, the word "meaning" has a distinct definition, that actors have their own kind of "meaning" to look for as they read.

Redfield is looking for the sort of meaning for the speech that is to be found in the effect it has on the other characters' actions within the play. The rugged Pyrrhus passage is important because of the acts it appears to impel Hamlet to perform in the future of the plot. Its dramatic meaning lies in the fact that as a consequence of watching this performance, Hamlet is "galvanized into action."

Moreover, Hamlet acts as a result of seeing that the Player King "is genuinely moved, genuinely distracted, genuinely tearful" as he speaks. That is, the famous words are not enough; it is the *act of speaking those words* in all its complexity of sights and sounds that has this effect, this meaning.

So Redfield is reading the text in order to imagine each act of the scene in physical detail. It's as if his working presumption (indeed the presumption of anyone working in practical terms in the theatre), is that the medium of the art, the raw material that both the playwright and his collaborators are working together to shape into a complete and resonant illusion, is the whole range of literal, specific human acts. And this includes the human act of speaking.

If the theatre is understood to be an art that is made by arranging specific acts—physical behavior, if you will—then it follows that, for the actor, drama will not be usefully understood as a genre of literature.

No one confuses sculpture and string quartets. They are equally valued arts independent of each other because they manipulate different materials using different techniques to produce distinct sorts of art objects. For the actor (and for philosophers from Aristotle to Suzanne Langer) literature and drama are also independent arts and for the same reasons—they work with different materials (language vs. visible and audible behavior); they work with those materials in different ways (the writer working alone vs. the elaborate collaborative procedures of the theatre); and they work to produce distinct art objects (a construction of words on a page vs. a story acted out in front of an audience by live performers.) In the theatre, drama isn't a genre of anything. Drama stands by itself.

The purpose of the special kind of reading that goes on in the rehearsal hall, then, is to imagine what a play must have—a completed story, articulated through physical behavior. Again, appealing to Aristotle's argument, the job of reading the text of a play for the stage is reading to imagine a seamless *mythos* for the performance to come.

CHAPTER 2

Illusion, Imagination, and Logic

The problem for the actor is a simple one, I should say the word again with a capital S, a Simple and profound problem . . . in the end and at the beginning, the actor is simply concerned that his audience believe.

—EDWARD PETHERBRIDGE

Artists who collaborate to create plays—the playwright, actors, director, designers, musicians—can claim all sorts of ambitions for their work. They can hope their plays will teach, or provoke, or offer reflection, escape, or insight. But theatre artists always have one job they must accomplish first, no matter what else they intend. Their work will come to nothing if they fail to persuade an audience to accept the story they are presenting on the stage. The first theatrical job is to create an illusion.

Edward Petherbridge knew this was his job when he was preparing to play Armado for the Royal Shakespeare Company. He described the problem as a simple and profound concern for the actor—"that his audience believe."[10]

Alright, but "belief" is a weighty word. "Believe" in what? What sort of "belief" leads to the dramatic illusion we must achieve before anything else?

When Samuel Taylor Coleridge was writing about the Shakespeare he saw in the early nineteenth century, he formed a phrase that has entered the language as a description of the state of mind a play creates in an audience. If a play is going to succeed, he wrote, the spectacle on the stage must lead its audience toward what he called a "willing suspension of disbelief."

That's a useful phrase for actors and directors to consider. In a practical sense, how is it done? How does an actor come to imagine a role so that it will eventually persuade an audience to accept its obvious artifice and go along with the theatre's agreeable lies?

It is helpful to set aside one thing that a dramatic illusion is not. It is not a performed delusion.

I once heard of an event staged by a company of politically motivated performance artists working in Paris. One evening they dressed in clothes that were not normal for them—evening wear—and took themselves out to an expensive restaurant patronized by people they despised, *le tout Paris*, the rich and famous of that rich and famous city. They took their seats, ordered lavishly, ate sumptuously, and acted in such a way that they seemed to fit in perfectly with the other diners enjoying themselves around them. But when the bill came, they angrily tore it up, stood on the table, breaking glasses and plates, and shouted accusations at the disconcerted diners around them to the effect that *they* were not there to eat and indulge themselves, they were actors. What they had done, they claimed, was to create an illusion.

Well, was it?

They were wearing "costumes," they were pretending, in a convincing way, that they were members of the *haute bourgeoisie*, and everybody around them had no reason to believe that they were not. They were skilled performers; everyone who saw them at dinner was successfully fooled by their performance. Isn't that a dramatic illusion?

Coleridge would claim that it was not, on two counts. First, the other diners, to say nothing of the manager of the restaurant, were not willing participants in the falsehood. They found their evening thoroughly spoiled, and, leaving the merits of the political argument aside, everybody agreed that they had had no choice in the matter.

Second, the performers in the restaurant were treated as if they were actual customers, and they certainly consumed actual food and broke actual plates worth actual money. They had lied about real things.

Coleridge is pointing out that an illusion is both something that spectators can choose to accept or reject as they wish, and that what a spectator is accepting is a "suspension of *dis*belief;" it is not a matter of being fooled into believing something false, then finding out that he or she has been lied to.

Obviously, there is a clear difference between events that are true and performed events that represent a fiction on a stage. Yet a problem remains. It is equally obvious that a work of fiction can be, in another sense of the word, "truthful." So in order to understand how a theatrical illusion works, actors need to sort out these two uses of the word, "true."

Writing about *The Tempest*, Coleridge offers this approach:

> Whatever ... tends to prevent the mind from placing itself, or being placed, gradually in that state in which the images have such negative reality for the auditor, destroys this illusion, and is dramatically improbable. The other excellencies of the drama besides this dramatic probability, as unity of interest, with distinctness and subordination of the characters, and appropriateness of style, are all, so far as they tend to increase the inward excitement, means toward accomplishing the chief end, that of producing and supporting this willing illusion.[11]

Coleridge's suggestion is that we distinguish between what he calls "positive" and "negative" reality. The "negative reality" Coleridge has in mind is a kind of "reality" that a spectator *knows* isn't actually true; nevertheless, he or she is willing to set aside that fact for a couple of hours in the theatre because the fiction, which everybody knows perfectly well *is* a fiction, is interesting enough to be worth the effort.

Aristotle tackles the same issue and offers another way of sorting out the two kinds of "reality" implicit in the concept of creating an illusion on the stage. In *The Poetics*, Aristotle draws a distinction between events that are true because they *did* happen and events that are convincing because they are presented in such a way that they manage to persuade people that they *could have* happened; that is, "actual reality" on the one hand—events, people, and objects we know to exist—and "virtual reality" on the other hand—events, people, and objects we can imagine *might* exist. The first, says Aristotle, is the stuff of recorded history. The second is what we use to make, among other things, plays.[12]

If actors, enacting the events and speaking the words from the playwright's text, can show fictional behavior that an audience comes to imagine (or "believe," if you will) *could* be happening, then we can have a dramatic illusion, a new "virtual reality" we must have for our play to succeed.

If you are reading the text as an actor, then, what should you look for if you are going to try to imagine a virtual reality for the stage?

We know perfectly well that virtual reality need not look or sound like actual reality. We don't believe in ghosts, but we'll happily accept the appearances of Hamlet's father on the battlements of Elsinore. We know that people on the street don't converse in iambic pentameter unrhymed, but one of the joys of going to the theatre is to hear Shakespeare's characters speak in beautifully structured and intensely distilled language. And it's certainly possible to accept five actors and a flag as the assembled chivalry of France.

Here, for example, is Peter Brook rehearsing his famous production of *A Midsummer Night's Dream*. Brook is in Stratford with the company of actors, discussing the set and costumes planned for the performance—bare white walls and, for the most part, clothes of no determined time or place:

> "The costumes," he (Brook) continues, "will say nothing." Only the Mechanicals' appearance will emphasize their "fixed occupation" and its nature, in juxtaposition with that of the court and the courtiers. "With a white background and a few objects," Brook tells the actors, "all the richness will have to come from the performing group." It will have to "paint the picture as it goes." Moreover, "literally illustrating the action is out." If Puck "says he is going," then "it is sufficient that he says it, and stands still." And, "when he says he is back, he is back." Once more, the exploration of the nature of theatrical illusion, and of the role of the imagination, including the audience's, beckons.[13]

Nothing in Brook's staging of the events in Shakespeare's story looked or sounded as if it were actual, yet the ability of this production to create an engaging virtual reality in the imaginations of people watching is a matter of theatrical history. Audiences knew they were watching fiction—the production was designed to see that they never forgot it. But they also chose to enter into that fiction, follow the story, and respond to the human situations represented there, at least in part, *because* of the way Brook and his company decided to enact the events indicated in the text.

Still, every dramatic illusion is fragile. Brook's audience might have felt that the blank walls and few objects weren't enough to create the illusion they wanted to see. Brook's huge success could have been a flop. Coleridge warns about those things that "prevent the mind from placing itself, or being placed, gradually in that state of mind" where the imaginative acceptance of a fiction can happen.

So what does an audience *need* to be willing to suspend their disbelief? Both Coleridge and Aristotle assert that plays must have what they both call dramatic probability, Coleridge placing it above all "the other excellencies of the drama."

Plays, and this is pointedly true for the texts of William Shakespeare, tend to be made up of extraordinary behavior, lavish activity, intense language, and concentrated events. Dramatic illusion requires that the extraordinary be made to seem probable, likely, a logical extension of what an audience already knows. Spectators, if they are going to "believe" the striking events they are watching, need to know what other events or conditions in the play made them come about; or, if they don't know while it's all going on, they need to have the confidence that, in time, they will come to discover the reasons the characters are behaving as they do.

These causes for action are as much a part of the fiction of the play as are the acts themselves. Coleridge and Aristotle are not looking for the playwright's "reasons" for having something happen, or the director's, or the actors', or the critic's reasons. Rather, what counts is the *characters'* apparent reasons behind each act, each gesture, each speech. The illusion arises, the "suspension of disbelief" can occur, when the audience is persuaded that every act they are watching has a logical cause from within the story, and that, in turn, each act will serve as a persuasive cause for consequences to follow.

There appears to be a paradox here, but practical experience proves it valid: An illusion succeeds when the theatre uses its artifice to appeal to an audience's sense of what seems logical. Spectators know perfectly well that adult brothers and sisters cannot look interchangeably alike, that victims' ghosts don't haunt the tents of rival kings, or that a magic staff is unlikely to bring down a masque of classical deities. But they are usually willing to suspend their disbelief in these impossibilities if, as they watch them and their logical causes and consequences, everything seems plausibly connected.

Dramatic probability was at the heart of Petherbridge's hope as he rehearsed Armado; could he imagine a way to make a believable logic manifest to his audience? Could he persuade them to suspend their disbelief by showing them how everything he did on stage had a specific cause and specific consequences within the action of the play?

CHAPTER 3

Improvising Shakespeare

The words must be found or coined or fresh-minted at the moment you utter them. They are not to be thought of as something which pre-exists in a printed text. In the theatre they must seem to find their life for the first time at the moment the actor speaks them. Because he needs them.[14]

—JOHN BARTON

In the theatre, most Shylocks behave in ways that provoke tragic sympathy in the audience. There have been others, however, wearing a red fright wig, perhaps, running around the stage spilling ducats and screeching in their frustration, who won belly laughs. Different Hamlets have seemed infinitely sensitive or gratuitously cruel by the time their stories have been revealed. Henry V has manipulated Catherine in one theatre, and Catherine has manipulated Henry V in the next. One Kate loses when she kneels to Petruchio, while another Kate rises finally victorious.

In each case, the words the actors speak needn't change. The structure of the playwright's plot is as it has always been. A unique *Hamlet, Henry V,* or *The Taming of the Shrew* means a faithful performance of the playwright's words and plot, but one that makes those familiar incidents seem probable and coherent in a new way. When the actors reveal a new dramatic logic, a persuasive new chain of causes and acts, the famous words from the text can suddenly seem "found or coined or fresh-minted."

Writing a script for a play, that is, choosing words for characters to speak, is unlike any other kind of writing. We have already seen how, within the theatre, the playwright is writing words for a form of art whose medium is not language but behavior. So the playwright, ironically enough, is an artist composing words for a work of art that is not, in essence, made out of words. In plays, words have a different function.

Professor Suzanne Langer is, again, helpful in this regard. In *The Dramatic Illusion*, she notes:

> Lines in a play are only the stuff of speeches; and speeches are only some of the acts which make drama. They are, however, acts of a special sort. . . . Verbal utterance is the overt issue of a greater emotional, mental and bodily response, and its preparation in feeling and awareness or in mounting intensity of thought is implicit in the words spoken. Speech is like the quintessence of action.[15]

Langer sorts out writing for the stage from all other kinds of artistic writing by proposing a specific relationship between the words of fictional speeches written by the playwright and the detailed action an audience will eventually see. Her argument is this: Since plays represent human acts on the stage, and since people, in actual life, usually speak *in response* to physical or mental events, speech on stage also should appear to be a reaction to something. And that "something" that causes the response should appear to be implicit in the language the character speaks. Therefore, every line should be written by the playwright as if there were a fictional cause, a virtual "preparation," which could logically impel the character to say those words at that moment in the action.

Much of the final play can be set out in explicit terms by the playwright, including the words of the speeches. However, remember that if the illusion is going to succeed, it's the *act* of speaking, the physical form and sound those words will take in performance, that has to appear to arise from the character's experience. That imaginary experience includes events and circumstances that the text can only suggest; the forces at work in the immediate situation; the physical reality of the place; the pressures of time; and the sights and sounds of every other speech and action. So no matter how gifted a writer the playwright is, most of the particular causes behind each act and speech will remain implicit only, that is, indicated, but incomplete on the page.

A successfully completed character, for example, Macbeth, will be performed by the actor in such a way that it appears as if Macbeth, on his own, chose the words he has to say, not as if Shakespeare did. Everybody involved understands that this effect is in the nature of the theatrical illusion itself. An audience is there to imagine that they are watching a fictional man talking, so the actor needs to do more than recite the actual playwright's words. If he wants the audience to accept his performance as a persuasive representation of a human being called Macbeth, he needs to show a completed illusion of the way speech really works: He needs to show a imaginary man who appears to be thinking, feeling, and responding to his own experience as he speaks his lines.

While they are preparing this illusion, then, actors need to learn to read their texts backwards, in a sense. They need to read the words; they also need to imagine those words as a "quintessence of action," finding their way back from every speech to the character's needs, thoughts, and sensations that might have provoked the act of speaking those words. Part of the actor's job is to decide, from all the elements in the action that are spelled out in the text and from those left only implicit, *why* Macbeth might choose to say that speech at that specific moment in the action. What *is* the specific "something" that might bring the speech about?[16]

In a recent interview, the English director Jonathan Miller explained his understanding of how this process of analysis and invention works in rehearsal:

> Can I say in a sense that my basic idea springs from one notion which comes not from the theatre, but from linguistic philosophy? It comes from a rather striking phrase by the Oxford philosopher, Peter Strawson . . . He said that it was not propositions which mean something but the people who mean things by the propositions they utter. And I think that in the theatre what one has is a series of texts very many of which are almost bereft of collateral instructions telling one what the characters are and what they mean by what they say. What you therefore have to do is improvise, and discover and

embody people or personalities who might convincingly and consistently have meant something by all the utterances which happen to be written down opposite their name in the texts which we have inherited from the past.[17]

This is Miller's understanding: The words in a script are supposed to appear to be the utterances of a fictional person. They are meant to be understood as an imaginary individual's response to a previous act or an existing circumstance in the world of the play. To be anything like actual life, the fictional speaker must seem to have something specific in mind as he or she chooses those words; the words of the speech must appear to hold a specific meaning *for the fictional speaker*. And this meaning may, or may not, be the same sort of meaning that the words themselves, standing on a page apart from the act of speaking, would convey.

We have already seen how a speech's dramatic "meaning" can be found in the events that the speech causes to happen later in the play. To achieve such a meaning for a speech, an actor has to "improvise" a plausible and coherent *intention* behind his or her character's act of speaking. A character must appear to want his or her words to mean a particular thing to other particular characters. A character must seem to want his or her speech to have a specific effect, to make other characters respond to these words in a particular way.

Given that, crucial questions in the search for a *dramatic* meaning for a speech emerge: "What could the character expect to convey, specifically, as they speak these words?", "To whom?", "In the hopes of accomplishing what?", "What is the character *intending to make happen* as he or she talks?"

Miller suggests that an actor must imagine a consistent series of fictional intentions behind those speeches and acts assigned to his or her character and must improvise the behavior that will make that coherence visible. In other words, a new character from Shakespeare's texts can be "improvised," beginning with a specific conception of what that character intends to make happen each time he or she acts.

By extension, a play as a whole is a succession of physical acts representing the behavior defining a number of characters, each appearing to act and speak in response to the events and circumstances bearing down on them. In order to create a dramatic illusion based on a probable logic, a theatre company must "improvise" virtual contexts and connecting intentions behind *all* of the acts performed by *all* of the characters.

It is in this sense, Jonathan Miller's sense, that we are calling the theatrical way of thinking about a text, *"improvising* Shakespeare." Improvising Shakespeare means learning to read the text in order to imagine a virtual impetus for each word in Shakespeare's language and every incident in his plot. It means presuming that the words for the stage could plausibly be spoken by a fictional person in response to a particular situation, to a particular act, or to a particular thought yet to be conceived. It means imagining that a character, as a fictional representation of a person made out of physical acts, can become believable when those acts are seen to grow out of an implied consciousness, a virtual (not actual) mind that can appear, if the audience can see convincing behavior on the stage, to be thinking, feeling, and choosing.

"Improvising Shakespeare" means inventing, and finding ways to reveal, the thinking of each fictional mind implicitly at work within the action of the play.

Here is an example of the idea. Laurence Olivier gave an interview to the BBC in which he described part of the rehearsal process for a production of *Macbeth* at Stratford:

> Another thing time gives you is more chance to think about things, to work things out in any Shakespearean tragedy. For instance, we worked it out that it was perfectly obvious that, as Lady Macbeth says about the king "If he had not resembled my father as he lay", Duncan was her father's brother, so that she was really in direct line of succession. And probably the moot, or whatever they were called in Scotland in those days, turned her down because she was only a snip of a girl. They said, "We can't give the crown to her, we'd better give it to the brother"; that happened constantly in those days. But she was in the direct line of succession, I'm sure. She then marries the splendid young Montgomery of the time and they would have shared the pillow with many an intimate thought, "Of course, dear, you're the fellow who ought to be the next king and, after all, I'm the daughter of the last one." When they first meet Lady Macbeth says to her husband, "Your face, my thane, is as a book, where men may read strange matters." They've talked about it and so when he tries to put it off, he says, "We will speak further"; it's something they both know about.[18]

In the text of *Macbeth*, Shakespeare explicitly indicates that these two people, Macbeth and Lady Macbeth, each respond to the idea of their accession to the throne of Scotland in conflicting ways. Macbeth hesitates, struggling with the moral consequences of his act and, once he's killed the king, is plagued with "fits" that torture his mind like "scorpions." Lady Macbeth, a woman of no less acuity than her husband, acts decisively. She seems uninterested in the conventional morality of her act (as long as she stays awake), dismissing Macbeth's thoughtful and accurately predicted concerns as the quavering of a coward. The actor's question is, what specific thoughts and intentions could plausibly drive this couple into the conflict so clearly laid out in the text?

The "improvisation" Olivier offers is this: What if Lady Macbeth's father and King Duncan were brothers (since the text suggests that the two men looked alike)? What if, when her father died, she had been passed over in the succession because she was "only a snip of a girl?" Lady Macbeth could plausibly believe that the crown of Scotland had been unjustly taken from her. She could logically feel that the crown was hers by right. In her mind, she isn't the usurper, Duncan is. She's the rightful heir, and Duncan is only another uncle who stepped in between an election and a prince's hopes. When the opportunity presents itself to right this wrong, she never hesitates, except, Olivier suggests, at the moment off stage when she recognizes Duncan's kinship to her father, because she sees herself as the principal victim in this story.

Macbeth has second thoughts, even if he knows his wife's claims of rightful ambition. He's no victim. He knows that Duncan has treated him generously and ruled well. Perhaps he feels that the "moot, or whatever they were called in Scotland in those days"—the legal authority who decided to take the crown from Lady Macbeth and give it to Duncan—were wise in their decision; "This Duncan hath borne his faculties so meek, hath been so clear in his great office, that his virtues will plead like angels . . . " He knows that *he* has no rightful claim to the throne, no matter what his wife might think. He has only a tempting idea, planted by his wife in conversations on their pillow and nurtured by his encounter with the witches.

Still, he acts. He kills the king. But he cannot finish the plan. It is Lady Macbeth, her mind unclouded by hesitations or a sense of having done wrong, who grabs the bloody daggers and stages the cover-up to the assassination. It's the courageous thing to do, from her point of view; she feels herself entirely in the right.

Given these imagined personal histories and thoughts, the conflict that will grow between the two characters can become inevitable and specific. As Olivier's suggestion led him to imagine particular behavior for one scene, that behavior will, in turn, suggest specific causes for the acts to follow in the course of the play. If Macbeth and Lady Macbeth have conflicting ideas about the justice of their plans, what specific form will their encounters after the murder take? Can you imagine, with Olivier's suggestion in mind, new ways to hear the lines, "Macbeth hath murdered sleep," "things without remedy should be without regard," "She should have died hereafter; there would have been time for such a word"? Try.

Olivier never claims to give us *the* meaning of the play, or even of the line Lady Macbeth utters about Duncan's appearance as he sleeps. Improvising Shakespeare is not an attempt to claim final solutions or paradigmatic interpretations that put all other critical analyses to rest. For all the talk of "definitive" versions of one role or another, actors have always known that other actors come along and use their own imaginations to recreate these characters over and over again. As David Garrick is supposed to have observed some 250 years ago, "actors write upon water . . ."

Olivier's improvisation is a suggestion for *a* plausible logic, one that appealed to his imagination, based on his close reading of the text. It was an idea, when pursued with his colleagues in rehearsal, that developed into a detailed conflict that could make the acts and words of the play seem coherently impelled by specific circumstances and behavior from within the action. It led, step by step, to a new theatrical illusion from this text by giving the actors, and, in turn, the audience, an imaginative and convincing logic at work behind the fictional behavior they were seeing.

This is the process of reading we are going to explore and practice. In rehearsal, one improvisation, based on a close reading of the text, leads to another and another. Eventually, a new *Macbeth*, a new *Taming of the Shrew, Henry V*, or a new *Merchant of Venice* may, in fact, appear.

PART TWO

Practice

CHAPTER 4

Where to Look

Monday, 13 October
Spent all morning rehearsing the first scene of HAMLET—four
hours—and it was a wonderful experience. It's really why I do this
job . . . for the satisfaction of having a really good rehearsal where
the excitement of discovery spreads from actor to actor.[19]
                                                    —Peter Hall's *Diaries*

The excitement of discovery *is* a wonderful experience in a rehearsal.
It is that experience of discovery that leads to the appearance of new
plays from inherited texts. Discovering, or imagining, a way a famous
work might come to make new sense as it is completed for the stage
is the way of thinking about Shakespeare's texts that we are trying to
explore. Hall's "excitement of discovery" is, in fact, what I mean by
"improvising Shakespeare."

There is a practical question, however: Where are these "discoveries" to be found? Where should you learn to look?

Remember what you're looking for: In order to complete a theatrical illusion for the stage, you need to imagine the play in terms of
acts of human behavior that are explicit, specific, and plausible to an
audience. As you study the words of dialogue and soliloquy in the
text, you're trying to picture what could be going on and what, in the
story, might be making it happen.

You can begin your search by looking for elements in the text that remind you of actual human behavior. A play represents human behavior by acting it out on stage (a play "imitates" it, to use Aristotle's word), so learn to look for signs of human action that you recognize. Do the characters do the sorts of things real people are likely to do?

Yes, of course they do. Among the elements of recognizable human behavior the playwright's language can suggest for the stage are these:

1. We've already seen how one person's act, speech, or gesture is often understood as a physical response to something someone else is doing. A playwright, working on an illusion of action, uses this characteristic of actual human behavior all the time. Scripts largely consist of a succession of actions and reactions for the stage.

Part of the actor's job, in turn, is to imagine the play in terms of such a succession of literal, visible behavior. Actors can discover a great deal, in the process of picturing the play in their imaginations, by improvising this chain of detailed physical action and reaction for the stage.

2. Real people's behavior is affected by the physical conditions surrounding it; where it happens—how that place looks, sounds, smells, and feels; what time it is—the hour, the day, the year, the time in a person's life; what the weather is; who else is present; what the occasion at hand is; and so on.

Actual behavior is conditioned by psychological, emotional, and spiritual contexts as well. The pressures people are working under clearly affect their behavior; so do their emotional situations. When a person does something or responds to somebody, what dangers, successes, joys, ambitions, irritations, or fears fill his or her thoughts?

In the theatre, an imaginary physical and emotional context for each action and reaction is an essential factor in the illusion we're trying to improvise. These virtual conditions that appear to affect the action of a moment have a name, a useful bit of theatrical jargon that has come down to us from the great Russian actor, teacher, and director, Stanislavski. A playwright can suggest, in both explicit and implicit terms, what he called the "given circumstances" for a scene. Reading Shakespeare's text and imagining a specific account of all the given circumstances at work in a particular incident is a very promising source of useful and playable ideas for the stage.

3. Real people often do things because they believe that by doing them, they will successfully accomplish something. The thing they choose to do is specifically intended to make something else happen next.

Sometimes real people choose correctly, and they get what they want. But real people's perceptions, interestingly enough, are usually subjective, only partial, and often inaccurate. So their choice of action may lead to a result they didn't intend or expect.

Still, we come to understand what a real person's behavior means to that person when we get him or her to answer the question, "What did you have in mind when you did *that?*"

Ask the same question of each character as you read. Trying to imagine every speech and act in the text as a tactic chosen by a character to accomplish a particular result within the story is another rich source for theatrical discovery. Again, the playwright can make that goal explicit or leave it unspoken. In either case, however, the illusion is that a character has a virtual mind hard at work, engaged in an action that is intentional. He or she seems to be choosing specific ways of acting in order to accomplish a specific result. Your imagining may uncover a mind fully capable of making crucial and revealing mistakes as well as one able to choose effectively. Looking for a character's plausible intentions always offers a wealth of possibilities for discovery and improvisation.

4. Actual people pursuing a goal often get surprised along the way. As they work to accomplish a particular end, they can learn something important they hadn't known before; accidents can happen; someone else, perhaps pursuing the same goal, can do something that throws them off track; or people can discover, in the course of their pursuit, that the goal isn't worth all the trouble they're going through to achieve it.

When they get a surprise, people have to adjust. They have to decide how they are going to respond to the change in what they know, what they believed, or what they face. Those can be among the most difficult decisions people have to make in their entire lives.

Plays often show characters making crucial discoveries in dealing with surprises or facing unexpected changes in circumstances. Then they show those characters making their adjustments, choosing how to respond, deciding specifically what they want to do next.

Those fictional decisions can be among the most revealing moments in a play. A character is truly established in the audience's imagination when they watch the character choosing how to act, deciding how to respond to surprising events and discoveries in a specific way. So finding and imaginatively exploring those moments of discovery and decision in a text are valuable things to do.

Still, it's good to remember that characters are *not* real people. They are artificial. They are artistic representations of people made out of acts deliberately selected and artfully arranged for an audience to watch and hear.

Experienced actors know that Shakespeare's artistic abstractions can engage the actor's imagination as productively as can his observations from life. So, as you read, you need to consider the artificialities of the text as closely as those elements in the text that reflect actual human experience:

1. Shakespeare was, of course, as richly gifted a poet as ever lived. His language, as language, remains unmatched in its ability to evoke sensation and significance. Both his craft and his invention as an artist of language astonish us.

But he was also an actor himself, and his writing suggests that he clearly understood the needs of his fellow actors as he wrote. The language is shaped so that it can be directly and acutely helpful to the theatrical search. A choice of word, a phrase or an image, a shift in meter, or a placement of stress can suggest specific ideas about a character's literal behavior and immediate motives. An actor needs to develop an ear for reading Shakespeare's ways of crafting language that direct the imagination toward the spoken action of a moment.

2. Among the artificialities of the construction of a play is the manipulation of time. Shakespeare's writing manages to shape both the virtual time of the story and the actual time of the performance in evocative ways. He chooses specific devices to compress a story covering days or years into a couple of hours in a theatre. He represents all kinds of fictional time on the stage, showing us inventive versions of historical time, of times of day and year, and of the ages of people's lives as his story unfolds.

He also designs the tempo of events and the rhythm of speech; the text suggests almost musical ways of organizing the time the play will occupy as it is performed.

All these manipulations of time can suggest useful ideas for the stage. On the one hand, the amount and kind of imaginary time the story depicts is an important given circumstance to consider as the actor pictures a character's actions and motives. On the other hand, the pace, the rhythms, the shifts of tempo in a speech, a physical act, a scene, and in the play as a whole can establish a pattern of time for the action, a pattern which can suggest even more appropriate and satisfying improvisations to an actor.

3. Finally, there is the whole idea of the construction of a plot. Plots are made when a playwright decides to select fictional incidents for the stage and assemble them in a certain order. In a play, things happen at a certain moment, in a certain context, and with certain consequences, all by design.

All the other elements in the text, both those that are drawn from common human experience and those that are the artificial conventions of the play, are made coherent by the structure of the plot, by the arrangement of events the playwright designs and indicates through dialogue. An actor or a director, learning to find that structure and imagining how and why this story could be put together as it is, can discover a theatrical logic behind each character's acts.

This way of thinking about Shakespeare's texts needs practice. In each of the chapters to follow, I will give you a scene to work on, one that has provoked actors to offer a number of contrasting improvisations, for each of these seven areas of exploration.

I will lay out the scene at first for you to read just as it stands. See what occurs to you as you read. Take notes; record questions and ideas as they flash across your mind. Don't edit your first reactions— they may turn out to be false starts, but they may also turn out to hold the germ of a new idea for the scene.

Then I'll take you back through the scene, asking specific questions which grow out of the dramatic characteristic I'm trying to isolate and explore in each case. I hope these questions will suggest your own improvisations as you read.

A word of advice: Take the time to *answer* the questions, either as you read by yourself, or, even better, as you read with somebody else. As Peter Hall said, the excitement of discovery spreads from actor to actor. One idea leads to another, either in one imagination, or, as in the real world of rehearsals, among a company of imaginations. The notion is that we are looking for a chain reaction of events. Each character enacts links in that chain. So, if possible, share the work of reading; each reader can imagine the specific behavior a particular character enacts to complete the logic informing the action of the scene.

The questions I am going to ask will lead you to consider and imagine details of the action. To be useful, your answers will have to be specific. Another seeming paradox is at work here; as a rule, the more precise and detailed an actor's questions and answers are, the freer the actor's imagination can become. If you choose a sharply defined solution to a mystery posed by the text, you'll find that more and more useful ideas will come for the mysteries to follow.

Try it yourself: "Romeo goes into Juliet's garden because he has fallen in love with her," may be true, as far as it goes, but as a specific improvisation for imagining the Balcony Scene it's pretty useless. It is so general a proposition that it suggests very little for the actor to do on stage except to moon about in an exhibition of stereotypical passion. An audience will never come to know a unique Romeo if you are satisfied with a version of the scene based on general descriptions of emotion.

But see what begins to come to mind when you start the scene asking detailed questions such as: What is the specific lay-out of this garden? Where are the trees, the plants, the paths, the walls, the other windows of the house? How did Romeo manage to get there? What obstacles did he run into? How do the Capulets keep their property secure? Dogs, perhaps? How does Romeo see? Where are the sources of light? Where are the other Capulets? Old Capulet? Tybalt? Why didn't they hear Mercutio bellowing about Rosaline outside the walls? Or did they? What if Romeo broke into the garden because he feels he has to prove to Juliet that he's capable of a good deal more than just kissing 'by the book'? What might happen in the moment when Romeo gives himself away? Or does he? What if he got caught? How might that come about, specifically? (After all, he's spying on the daughter of the Capulet family as she's getting ready for bed.) How is Juliet dressed? How will the action be colored by the fact that the Friar mentions that Juliet customarily shares her bed with the Nurse? What if she were savoring the sensation of danger as she wonders aloud about Romeo? What if she'd had a delightful time defying her parents by using the party (where she is supposed to be considering the County Paris) to flirt with a strange young man in a mask? Has she suddenly discovered that she's started something that's *really* dangerous? What might she be thinking? What might she intend? What might she hope for, here and now? What does she discover? At what moment in the scene does she make her specific discoveries? What might she imagine she's going to do as a result? And what does Romeo discover? Why do you suppose he feels the need to speak in florid metaphors at the beginning of the scene and is content to speak simply at the end? What might have changed? When might it have changed? What could Juliet *do* to make it change?

Any ideas?

The point is, generalities won't help much in a rehearsal. An actor and a director need to find specific ideas which can lead to specific acts. Generalities tend to let theatrical imaginations off the hook. So make yourself think only in precisely defined answers to concrete questions.

"Shakespeare gives the actor no adjectives," wrote the American actress and teacher, Uta Hagen; "Goody!"[20] This is more good advice. State your sharply focused answers in terms of action—what it is, where it comes from, and what it causes. Use verbs, not adjectives.

You might say something like, "Hamlet is profoundly shaken by the appearance of the ghost of his father." But while that conclusion *describes* Hamlet well enough, it also reduces him to an adjective, "shaken." All that answer suggests is an image of somebody who *is* something, not of somebody who *does* something. A character's state of being is not, by itself, an act which leads to a new action.

But what if you decide that Hamlet begins the scene by trying to escape the ghost's commands? That's an active answer. "Try to escape" is a verb you can imagine a character doing. Or how might your Hamlet behave if you chose that he were using the ghost to justify the regicide he has already decided, secretly, to do? "Use the ghost" is also active. Jonathan Pryce startled his audiences by playing this scene alone. Both voices came from the single throat of a Hamlet writhing helplessly on the floor. That compelling improvisation might have arisen from an answer such as, "Hamlet is *exorcising* the ghost from his own tortured mind, from his own 'prophetic soul' ."

In each case, the reason a verb in the actor's answer is particularly useful is because it inevitably leads to another useful question: *How* does the character go about it? In answering the question "how," specific new acts can be imagined and chosen for the stage. Verbs can suggest useful ideas for action. Adjectives rarely do.

Next, you'll find that each of the questions asks you to reason your way through a mystery posed by a moment in the text. Remember that audiences need probability. So make sure your answers convince you of their logic, their plausibility. Could you, as a member of an audience, accept the answer you are giving? Could you suspend your disbelief at the completion for the story you are proposing? If it is illogical and implausible to you, so will it be to an audience. The illusion cannot be achieved without achieving the appearance of likelihood. Test your answers against that marker.

Finally, trust your imagination, your own ability to make engaging discoveries. Shakespeare's work is so encrusted with intimidating precedent, both from scholars and from previous performances, that even experienced theatre people can feel frozen in their tracks, their imaginations paralyzed by the thought of all the talent and intelligent analysis that has gone before.

But we are working from the premise that every play is only beginning to reach its theatrical fulfillment every time reading and rehearsing begin. Every production can become a voyage of discovery, and, as Peter Hall said, is capable of being a profound fulfillment, a joy, and the reason for this work.

So as you study the chapters that follow, demand a lot of your imagination. Make sure every step of your own improvisation is focused, sharp, active, and seems plausible to you. Fresh, surprising, and believable new scenes from Shakespeare are waiting to be discovered.

CHAPTER 5

Physical Action

There is no character. There is no one there. It is only you, dear reader, or dear actor-as-reader. It is an illusion caused by the syllogism, "If A then B." Character, as Aristotle told us, is action.[21]
—DAVID MAMET

Events on stage, acted so they show convincing fictions, can be evocative things. They can make audiences imagine, reflect on, argue with, laugh at, cry about, or rise in righteous wrath at what appears to be going on. But what an audience is watching, strictly speaking, is simply an arrangement of physical action. Plays are made out of such things as mixing a drink, uttering a remark, shooting a pistol, having breakfast, throwing goloshes, hiding under a table, or picking up a skull—bits of literal behavior.

When I pointed this out to a class of student actors, one young man rose in indignation. "You mean that's IT?" he protested.

Yes. That's it. And that's a great deal.

Physical action for the stage is any specific human behavior created for an audience to see and hear. A kiss, a sword fight, a poisoning, a prank, a dance, or a punch in the nose is obviously a physical action we could watch as actors played it out. But, remember, so is a speech. It, too, is an act one character is physically doing, usually with another character physically engaged in the behavior of listening and reacting to what is said. And none of this physical action exists when you begin to read the page. It is waiting to be imagined and performed.

Remember, too, that for any physical act to make to sense to an audience, for the illusion of action to succeed, that act must appear to have been caused. So learn to think of each act in a play as a *re*action; something the audience can see and hear happen before the act in question must seem to have brought it about. By the same token, each act must seem to have physical consequences; as it appeared to be caused by a previous act, now it becomes one cause for acts to follow.

When you try to develop a detailed picture of the physical action for a scene, then, you need to begin to imagine a *chain* of physical acts, including the acts of speaking the playwright's words. The illusion requires that every "link" in that chain could plausibly be caused by an event the audience can literally see or hear before, and each one could plausibly cause acts and speeches yet to come. As David Mamet observed, the theatrical illusion depends on the "syllogism, if A, then B."

This means that your first job, "actor-as-reader," is to imagine, as you read, a plausible *succession* of detailed physical actions that might be engaging and convincing enough to appear on the stage.

Consider this scene from *Romeo and Juliet:*

ACT I

Scene i
(A public place)

Enter SAMPSON *and* GREGORY, *armed with swords and bucklers.*

SAMPSON
Gregory, o' my word, we'll not carry coals.

GREGORY
No, for then we should be colliers.

SAMPSON
I mean, an we be in choler we'll draw.

GREGORY
Ay, while you live, draw your neck out o' the collar.

SAMPSON
I strike quickly, being moved.

GREGORY

But thou are not quickly moved to strike.

SAMPSON

A dog of the house of Montague moves me.

GREGORY

To move is to stir; and to be valiant is to stand:
therefore, if thou art moved, thou run'st away.

SAMPSON

A dog of that house shall move me to stand: I will take the
wall of any man or maid of Montagues.

GREGORY

That shows thee a weak slave; for the weakest goes to the
wall.

SAMPSON

True; and therefore women, being the weaker vessels, are
ever thrust to the wall: therefore will I push Montague's
men from the wall and thrust his maids to the wall.

GREGORY

The quarrel is between our masters and us their men.

SAMPSON

'Tis all one, I will show myself a tyrant: when I have
fought with the men I will be cruel with the maids, and cut
off their heads.

GREGORY

The heads of the maids?

SAMPSON

Ay, the heads of the maids, or their maidenheads; take it in
what sense thou wilt.

GREGORY

They must take it in sense that feel it.

SAMPSON

Me they shall feel while I am able to stand: and 'tis known
I am a pretty piece of flesh.

GREGORY

'Tis well thou art not fish; if thou hadst thou hadst been poor-John. Draw thy tool; here comes two of the house of Montague.

SAMPSON

My naked weapon is out: quarrel, I will back thee.

GREGORY

How! turn thy back and run?

SAMPSON

Fear me not.

GREGORY

Nay, marry: I fear thee!

SAMPSON

Let us take the law of our sides; let them begin.
I will frown as I pass by; and let them take it as they list.

SAMPSON

Nay, as they dare. I will bite my tongue at them; which is a disgrace to them if they bear it.

Enter ABRAHAM *and* BALTHASAR.

ABRAHAM

Do you bite your thumb at us, sir?

SAMPSON

I do bite my thumb, sir.

ABRAHAM

Do you bite your thumb at us, sir?

SAMPSON

Is the law of our side if I say ay?

GREGORY

No.

SAMPSON

No, sir, I do not bite my thumb at you, sir; but I bite my thumb, sir.

GREGORY

Do you quarrel, sir?

ABRAHAM

Quarrel, sir! no, sir.

SAMPSON

If you do, sir, I am for you: I serve as good a man as you.

ABRAHAM

No better.

SAMPSON

Well, sir.

GREGORY

Say better: here comes one of my master's kinsmen.

SAMPSON

Yes, better, sir.

ABRAHAM

You lie.

SAMPSON

Draw, if you be men. Gregory, remember thy swashing blow.

(They fight.)

Enter BENVOLIO.

BENVOLIO

Part, fools! put up thy swords; you know not what you do.

(Beats down their swords.)

Enter TYBALT.

TYBALT

What art thou drawn among these heartless hinds?
Turn thee, Benvolio, look upon thy death.

BENVOLIO

I do but keep the peace: put up thy sword,
Or manage it to part these men with me.

TYBALT

What, drawn, and talk of peace! I hate the word
As I hate hell, all Montagues, and thee:
Have at thee, coward!

(They fight.)

Enter several of both Houses, who join the fray; then enter CITIZENS
with clubs.

1 CITIZEN

Clubs, bills, and partisans! Strike! Beat them down! Down
with the Capulets! Down with the Montagues!

Enter CAPULET *in his gown, and* LADY CAPULET.

CAPULET

What noise is this? Give me my long sword, ho!

LADY CAPULET

A crutch, a crutch! Why call you for a sword?

CAPULET

My sword, I say! Old Montague is come,
And flourishes his blade in spite of me.

Enter MONTAGUE *and* LADY MONTAGUE.

MONTAGUE

Thou villain Capulet! Hold me not, let me go.

LADY MONTAGUE

Thou shalt not stir a foot to seek a foe.

Enter PRINCE, *with* ATTENDANTS.

PRINCE

Rebellious subjects, enemies to peace,
Profaners of this neighbor-stained steel,
Will they not hear? What, ho! you men, you beasts,
That quench the fire of your pernicious rage
With purple fountains issuing from your veins,
On pain of torture, from these bloody hands
Throw your mistemper'd weapons to the ground,
And hear the sentence of your moved prince.

Three civil brawls, bred of an airy word,
By thee, old Capulet and Montague,
Have thrice disturb'd the quiet of our streets;
And made Verona's ancient citizens
Cast by their grave beseeming ornaments,
To wield old partisans in hands as old,
Canker'd with peace, to part your canker'd hate:
If ever you disturb our streets again,
Your lives shall pay the forfeit of the peace.
For this time, all the rest depart away:
You, Capulet, shall go along with me;
And, Montague, come you this afternoon,
To know our further pleasure in this case,
To old Free-town, our common judgment place.
Once more, on pain of death, all men depart.

Shakespeare's scenes are often compact chains of action—a lot of things happen very fast. Profound changes in a situation develop quickly. So, to begin the process of improvising a plausible and interesting plan for the physical action in a scene, it's often useful to ask, how long and elaborate a chain of events are we talking about?

Compare the first incident in this opening scene of *Romeo and Juliet* to the last: The first piece of literal behavior indicated in the text is that two armed servants of the House of Capulet complain about their work, a complaint that leads them to indulge in word games. The last event is the Prince threatening citizens of Verona with death if they fail to leave the scene of a disturbance he has just (barely) been able to silence. Therefore, in these few lines, you have to show a convincing progress of incidents that goes from a scene of two servants procrastinating to the sights and sounds of deadly warnings in the aftermath of a riot.

Every physical act you imagine and select for your improvisation must be an act that could be a plausible link between those two stage pictures. If you're successful, you'll also choose a chain reaction of literal acts that might surprise an audience, one that engages and refreshes their imagination as well as appealing to their sense of what's reasonable.

Read through the scene again. Answer the questions I ask about the scene in specific and detailed terms. Ask further questions of your own—and answer them precisely as well. See if an interesting improvisation based on the physical activity of the scene begins to emerge in your imagination:

ACT I

Scene i
(A public place)

What "public place?" What do people in your imagining of the Verona of this play come here to physically do? Could it be an open-air market where people compete to sell fish, vegetables, furniture repair, stolen watches, or sex? Could you imagine a plaza where civic ceremonies are performed (the Prince mentions the citizens' "grave beseeming ornaments . . .")? Is it a place where people gather to hear the workings of their government? What human behavior might you *expect* to be going on here under normal conditions?

What characters will you put in this place? What will you have them physically do? Will you have Sampson and Gregory enter an empty place, or will they be entering a place filled with characters going about the sort of activities everyone expects to go on there? Could the normal life of the city be underway before Gregory and Sampson arrive? Imagine that activity in specific detail.

(A note here about the stage directions: "Enter" in this text may or may not mean the physical appearance of the character on the scene. Characters regularly talk about the entering character as if they had been there long before a printed stage direction says they "Enter." Characters might be doing lots of things within the scene before the playwright has them begin to speak. In each case, the physical presence and specific acts of each character who doesn't have lines at the moment are as important to imagine as the action of characters who do. So are the effects their presence and behavior could have on the other characters, speaking or nonspeaking, who are part of the scene.)

In any case, we know there is going to be a bloody riot; at some point, we have to imagine rioters, a "public" for this public place. Each of them has to have his or her things to do here, his or her own time or reasons for entering or leaving this scene. That's for you to improvise as well.

Enter SAMPSON *and* GREGORY, *armed with swords and bucklers.*

Where do you suppose Gregory and Sampson appear to be headed? They seem to be returning from some sort of chore for the House of Capulet. Is that what you imagine? What was their mission? How might their behavior grow out of their assigned task?

They are armed. What specific kinds of weapons will you choose for them? The stage directions mention "Swords and bucklers" (which are small shields) but the scene has been successfully played with a wide range of weaponry, from rapiers to tire irons. Choose your weapons (as they say), and, more important, choose a convincing dramatic logic that requires those particular weapons.

How will you have them carry their arms? As if they habitually wore weapons? As if they were issued arms because things are particularly tense in Verona right now? (We are about to see the third brawl, after all.) Do they carry them as if they, as servants, were proud to be entrusted with arms? Could they have stolen them? What might their physical behavior suggest about their role as fighters for the Capulets?

SAMPSON

Gregory, 'o my word, we'll not carry coals.

What physical event might make Sampson interrupt his work at this particular moment? And in this particular place?

Might they literally be carrying coals? There is to be a feast tonight at the Capulets, and that means cooking fuel will be required. How do you picture two men wearing "swords and bucklers" would go about the labor of lugging coal through the streets?

Or might Sampson be using coals as a general metaphor for his life of drudgery? If so, what is the specific physical activity you'll have him break off in order to register his complaint?

GREGORY

No, for then we should be colliers.

Gregory is agreeing with Sampson. He, too, is choosing to break off work, perhaps; work he also describes as lugging coal. What will your Sampson do that persuades Gregory to take a break at this time and place? Need it be Sampson's act that is the catalyst? Could something happen to Gregory independent of Sampson's remark? Can you imagine someone else in the place whose behavior has this specific effect? Try.

Sampson is getting it into his head to try a pun. What physical incident on the stage might plausibly lead Sampson to bring up a new thought?

(Another general observation: As you are reading, whenever you see that a character has words that indicate that he or she is changing the subject, mark it. A change of the subject in a speech, even a small one, means a change in the character's apparent thinking. Logically, *something* must happen to make the mind change direction. Look for a probable cause.)

SAMPSON
I mean, an we be in choler, we'll draw.

For whose benefit is this joke? Or boast? For Gregory's? What might Gregory have done to provoke Sampson to try a wisecrack at this point? Could Sampson's riposte be for someone else's benefit? Whose? What might he, or she, have done to stimulate this attempt at humor?

Does Sampson deliver the pun as if he thought it was funny? Does Gregory receive it as if it were funny to him? If you choose to have other people about, what do they hear? What does Sampson's stab at comedy cause them to do? Laugh, perhaps? Or groan? Or throw something at him?

Sampson says he'll "draw" something—his weapon, presumably. What caused him to think he needed to mention fighting at this moment? What might he do physically to make his intentions clear to the person he wishes to impress?

What might happen that could drive Gregory to respond as he does, with a pun of his own?:

GREGORY
Ay, while you live, draw your neck out o' the collar.

How do you imagine this line is said? Might it sound like sarcasm brought about by Sampson's showing off? Could it be directed at some member of the "public" who had reacted nervously to Sampson's implicit threat? Can you imagine a warning to Sampson that he's about to go too far?

How will Gregory's speaking of these words provoke the next line, which, on the face of it, could seem to be a *non sequitur*? Or could

Sampson's line be an answer to an act he sees rather than hears? What act can you imagine might make him say:

SAMPSON

I strike quickly, being moved.

Whom could Sampson be talking to? Gregory is a possibility, of course. But is that your only plausible choice?

What is his meaning? Could his speaking sound like a threat? A boast? A promise? How might he act to make sure his message gets through? And, specifically, to whom?

GREGORY

But thou are not quickly moved to strike.

How do you imagine this response? Might Gregory be calling Sampson's bluff? Might he be entertaining himself at Sampson's expense? Or entertaining someone else? Who? What if Gregory were jumping up to protect himself from a sudden burst of volatile temper from Sampson? What if Gregory were laughing? What if he were stepping in between Sampson and a hot tempered citizen? Or could he say these words in a way that suggested that he thought he and Sampson had better get back to work? No matter which reading you imagine, your choice should answer this question: What literal event could cause Gregory to respond in that way?

Sampson is about to bring up the enemies of their house, the Montagues. What event brings up this new subject? The general situation of tension between the two families might seem to be reason enough, but what makes Sampson choose to mention his master's enemies at *this* moment? For example, what might happen if some member of the Montague household put in an appearance? What might he (or she) be doing?

SAMPSON

A dog of the house of Montague moves me.

GREGORY

To move is to stir; and to be valiant is to stand:
therefore, if thou art moved, thou run'st away.

SAMPSON

A dog of that house shall move me to stand . . .

Gregory is talking in general terms about Sampson's claims of bravery; Sampson continues his specific threats against the Montagues. They are talking at cross purposes. What could be happening to make them do so?

Are you going to put any Montagues within earshot? Which ones? A Montague maid, perhaps?:

SAMPSON   (Continued)
    . . . I will take the wall of any man
or maid of Montagues.

Again, new subjects are introduced into the exchange: The courtesy of "taking the wall"—an important piece of etiquette in an age when slops were dumped out of windows onto the streets below—and the notion that the "maids" of the Montague family, as well as the men, are fair game in Sampson's eyes.

Both "taking the wall" and insulting the maids of the Montagues are ways of picking a fight. What immediate, on-stage event might happen to move Sampson to the point of proposing specific challenges? After all, just minutes ago he was only taking a break from his chores.

At any rate, Gregory doesn't seem to be very impressed. Or is he? What could he have seen? How might that immediate sight make him speak the words:

GREGORY
That shows thee a weak slave; for the weakest goes to the
wall.

SAMPSON
'True; and therefore women, being the weaker vessels, are
ever thrust to the wall: therefore will I push Montague's
men from the wall and thrust his maids to the wall.

GREGORY
The quarrel is between our masters and us their men.

What might happen to drive Sampson's threats into the sexual realm? What might occur that could make Sampson add bragging about his skill as a lover to his boasts as a fighter?

As soon as sex comes into the conversation, Gregory abruptly reminds Sampson that the fight is between the men of the two houses.

The women are not part of it. How might that line sound? As a warning? Delighting in Sampson's machismo? As an attempt to cool Sampson down? As a reaction to a threatening response from some citizens? As a response to something a visible Montague maid might have done? Choose.

SAMPSON
'Tis all one, I will show myself a tyrant . . .

To whom? Whom might Sampson be addressing as he promises to impose his will on all the Montagues?

Could something happen to make Sampson explain himself as he goes on?:

SAMPSON   (Continued)
. . . When I have fought
with the men, I will be civil with the maids—I will cut off
their heads.

Specifically, what sort of physical reactions can you imagine this inflammatory threat might provoke? (Remember, all during this scene, we are imaging a chain of events that lead from a peaceful situation to a bloody riot. Could this moment of bragging be one of the important steps in stirring up the emotions of everyone involved toward the flash point of chaos the Prince has to quell?)

Could it be Sampson's speech alone that causes Gregory's riposte? How would each man behave if that were the case? Might he be responding to the reactions these words stir up in a crowd? Make those crowd responses, if that's what you choose, specific in your mind's eye.

GREGORY
The heads of the maids?

SAMPSON
Ay, the heads of the maids, or their maidenheads; take it in what sense thou wilt.

Again, Shakespeare wrote inflammatory sexual humor for Sampson, and he had Sampson invite a "thou" to make sense of it. "Thou" is, of course, the singular pronoun. To what individual might his remark be made? Gregory might be your first choice, and that would make sense. But can you imagine some other individual in the scene who might be the target of this comment? Who could that be? How might he, or she, react to Sampson's innuendo?

If you choose Gregory, his answer might become a simple clarifying response. What might Gregory's response become if Sampson were hurling his jibe at someone else?

GREGORY
They must take it in sense that feel it.

Do you suppose Gregory says this line in a way that might cool someone off? What if he spoke the line in such a way that it could plausibly encourage Sampson to make even more insulting boasts?

The result of Gregory's assertion is, in fact, further coarse bragging. Do you suppose this is the response Gregory expected? Might we see him behave as though Sampson's vulgarity surprised him? Amused him? Frightened him?:

SAMPSON
Me they shall feel while I am able to stand: and 'tis known
I am a pretty piece of flesh.

Sampson evidently wants someone to admire his sexual ambitions and physical endowments. Who might that be? Gregory? Do you hear this remark as a smutty secret between two servants? Someone else? Who? What specific reaction might that provoke? How might that reaction make Gregory debunk Sampson so sharply, as he does when he says:

GREGORY
'Tis well thou art not fish; if thou hadst thou hadst been
poor john—

Reading Shakespeare often seems to be a matter of reading footnotes. In this case, the phrase "poor john" will probably send you to the bottom of the page, where you'll discover that "poor john" was a colloquial expression for salted and smoked hake or some other common fish available to feed poor people in Shakespeare's day.

Footnotes for these plays illustrate Jonathan Miller's thoughts about the meaning of propositions and utterances in the theatre. A footnote typically gives you useful, but general, meanings of the words, not an immediate and particular meaning intended by the character we are trying to imagine saying those words. The actor has to find a way to make Gregory's intended meaning—the response he is trying to provoke—clear whether or not the audience gets the reference to smoked fish.

In this case, Gregory could be responding to Sampson's sexual braggadocio. But what might his "message" be? How might he *use* this comparison between Sampson's anatomy and a smoked trash fish to convey his meaning? To whom might he deliver that message? Again, is Sampson your only choice?

Sampson has no words to answer Gregory's insult. Might he react physically?

Whatever that response is, it is interrupted, as you can see when Gregory suddenly changes subject in the middle of his line. What interrupts it? What physical event could make Gregory break off and say:

GREGORY   (Continued)
     . . . Draw thy tool;

Which "tool?" Could Sampson, given the subject of the last remarks, misunderstand? If so, how might each character involved respond to the misunderstanding? Might that behavior of misunderstanding be a cause for Gregory to explain:

GREGORY   (Continued)
. . . here comes two of the house of Montagues.

As I noted above, Shakespearean editors are notoriously inconsistent in the matter of entrances and exits. Some texts, such as the one I've cited here, save the word "ENTER" until a new character begins speaking. Others state that Abraham and Balthasar come in at this point because Gregory mentions that they have arrived.

These inconsistencies leave actors and directors free to imagine other times when Abraham and Balthasar might appear on the scene. What we must take from the text, however, is that this is the moment when Gregory first vocally responds to their presence. So ask what occurrence might make him speak up now.

Where might Abraham and Balthasar come from? Where might they appear to be headed? What could they be here, in this "public place," to do? How will they go about doing it?

Evidently, Sampson's first response to seeing the Montagues is to draw his weapon:

SAMPSON
My naked weapon is out:

But, remembering your earlier choices about which weapons he is carrying and how he wears them, *how* might he draw it? And what makes him need to tell Gregory in words that he has drawn it? Can't Gregory see for himself? Imagine behavior to explain that way of acting in this situation.

What might the Montague be doing that makes the Capulet servants think, immediately, of fighting? Or might someone else's act be the spark?

If you have chosen to have this public place filled with the public going about their own business, what will each of them do when a weapon appears? If you imagine this scene set in the period of rapiers, for example, a long sharp blade suddenly whipped out by an overexcited servant of limited skill might well clear a space rather quickly, with all sorts of interesting consequences in a crowd. And how might that response to the weapon specifically impel Sampson to go on to say:

SAMPSON   (Continued)
. . . quarrel, I will back thee.

A few words ago, Sampson seemed to be the one ready to pick a fight. Now he seems to be passing the responsibility back to Gregory. What might have happened to bring about this change of heart? (Remember to think in terms of literal acts, not general qualities of character.)

GREGORY
How! Turn thy back and run?

SAMPSON
Fear me not.

GREGORY
Nay, marry: I fear thee!

What might Abraham and Balthasar be doing while this exchange is going on? Are they aware of it, responding to it? How? Could Gregory and Sampson be saying this before the Montague men spot them? Is that likely, once a weapon has been drawn? If so, what specific events could make it plausible?

Since Gregory is making a point of Sampson's cowardice, what might Sampson be doing in addition to talking to provoke the remark?

Who is Gregory's audience? For whom is he speaking? For Sampson? For somebody in the crowd? For the Montague men? How will you have each person who perceives this exchange physically respond to it?

Could it be that response that leads Sampson to bring up a new idea? How will you make the introduction of the legalities of the situation the next logical step in the progression of events that leads to the riot?

SAMPSON

Let us take the law of our sides; let them begin.

GREGORY

I will frown as I pass by; and let them take it as they list.

SAMPSON

Nay, as they dare . . .

These two men had been at odds a few lines ago, bragging and embarrassing each other; now they are co-conspirators in a scheme that will legally protect them as they start a fight. Gregory changes from attacking Sampson to agreeing to his scheme. What on-stage incident could account for this change?

If the talk suddenly changes from two Capulet men chiding each other to two Capulet men making a tactical decision to start a fight with two Montagues, how might that change affect everybody else within earshot? What might listeners do if they heard Gregory suddenly agree to begin a brawl with the Montagues?

What happens to Gregory's frown? Somehow, the first attempt at picking a fight by making a face (what sort of face?) comes to nothing. Gregory's frown has only one result in the text—moving Sampson on to the more inflammatory gesture of biting his thumb. What visible reaction could that frown provoke? How could that reaction specifically tempt Sampson to try *his* luck?

SAMPSON   (Continued)
. . . I will bite my thumb at them; which is
a disgrace to them if they bear it.

What is this insulting gesture? We have lots of insulting gestures
of our own time that might be provocative, but they don't involve
thumb biting, and our gesture might seem innocuous to someone
from another culture. Again, it's not the gesture itself that provokes
the response, it's the meaning the person making the gesture has in
mind that counts. So invent a gesture that involves thumb biting and
that has the visibly plausible effect of insulting, in a very specific
way, the people toward whom it is directed.

How might each person who sees the gesture physically respond
to it? You only know that part of Abraham's response is to ask a precise question:

ABRAHAM
Do you bite your thumb at us, sir?

But what is the physical activity surrounding that question? What
other reactions might have been touched off by the thumb gesture?

How might he ask that question? Abraham's speaking has one
clear effect; it makes Sampson retreat into an evasive generality:

SAMPSON
I do bite my thumb sir.

What other immediate physical effects could his way of speaking bring about? For example, what might happen next if Sampson
was compelled to repeat the gesture?

ABRAHAM
Do you bite your thumb at us, sir?

What behavior does Abraham's exact repetition of the words of
his previous line suggest to you?

The text gives you one of those reactions. Abraham's speaking
drives Gregory and Sampson into a conference:

SAMPSON
Is the law of our side if I say ay?

GREGORY
No.

How, physically, could Sampson and Gregory get away from everyone in order to discuss the situation? Do they have to succeed? Might some people in the scene overhear this exchange? What will this conspiracy drive those who are aware of it to do? Each of them?

> SAMPSON
>
> No, sir, I do not bite my thumb at you, sir;

What visible reactions to this retreat could impel Sampson to go on:

> SAMPSON (Continued)
>
> . . . but I bite my thumb, sir.

And, again, what physical responses to Sampson's line might make Gregory decide to go on the attack?:

> GREGORY
>
> Do you quarrel, sir?

How might Abraham physically react now that he is the one who is being asked challenging questions?

> ABRAHAM
>
> Quarrel, sir! no, sir.

Imagine the activity possible for each character during this exchange of taunts. What might Balthasar be doing as Abraham talks? How could any witness you imagine react to the impending flare-up? What, in the way Abraham responds, or in one of the reactions to that response, could prompt Sampson to jump in and say:

> SAMPSON
>
> If you do, sir, I am for you:

This must provoke some sort of physical response from the Montagues. For example, Balthasar might laugh in Sampson's face. Can you think of a more surprising response that might plausibly provoke Sampson to go on to say:

> SAMPSON (Continued)
>
> . . . I serve as good a man as you.

You might see this as Sampson treading on dangerous ground. The masters of the two warring houses have not yet been mentioned, and they are men of importance in this town, "alike in dignity," the

Chorus might suggest. How would the mention of these impressive figures physically affect each hearer? Could this be the moment when the stakes in the fight begin to get high? If so, what physical behavior might result?

How might Abraham react to Sampson's taunt about the valor of Old Montague? What makes him speak in a way that allows the Capulets a safe retreat if they want to take it? Or could he be physically offering a challenge when he says:

ABRAHAM

No better.

Abraham seems to be drawing a line. If anyone says that Capulet is a better man than Montague, they'll fight. The Montagues will, out of courtesy or for the sake of civic peace, accept a claim of equal worth between the two leaders. But no one can claim superiority.

Is there a moment of suspense here? Does the public (if you imagine one) hold their breath as they wait for the Capulet response? Will Gregory and Sampson cross the line or not?

The effect of Abraham's speaking is to make Sampson choose to speak these temporizing words:

SAMPSON

Well, sir.

What if the threat of a fight were about to blow over? How would Sampson's retreat make everyone who sees it behave? Could you see people relax? Might they return to their normal occupations? What could happen to make this moment of ambiguity seem as if a brawl has narrowly been avoided?

If you choose this moment to be a brief pause, a breath of peace, something has to happen to make Gregory break it off. Specifically, what could it be? What could drive Gregory to say:

GREGORY

Say better: here comes one of my master's kinsmen.

Who? The next Capulet with lines will be Tybalt. It's reasonable to propose that Gregory has spotted him. Where could Tybalt be coming from? Where might he seem to be headed? What could he be doing before this fight interrupts him?

What on-stage event could make it likely that these two servants would start a brawl in order to please their master's cousin? What could Abraham, Gregory, Balthasar, or members of the citizenry be physically doing that would suggest to the Capulet men that they will gain favor by publicly embarrassing the servants of the House of Montague? What might Tybalt do to provoke this behavior?

Once again, don't be satisfied with an answer that suggests that since Mercutio calls Tybalt "the prince of cats" he is hot tempered; a character-label ["hot tempered"] is not an action an audience can see. Imagine some specific *activity* that, when an audience watches it, will provide a credible and specific stimulus for what is to come.

At this point Sampson is evidently responding to some event when he follows Gregory's command and says:

SAMPSON

Yes, better, sir.

This is the remark that sets off the conflagration. Sampson decides to cross the line Abraham laid down. How could Sampson speak these words and behave physically to both plausibly and surprisingly lead to the riot that is to come? What, for example, might Sampson be doing with his drawn weapon as he speaks?

What can you imagine each hearer's physical response might be to this direct insult to Old Montague? Don't leave anyone out in your imagining.

ABRAHAM

You lie.

SAMPSON

Draw, if you be men.

Sampson's line indicates that the one thing Abraham and Balthasar do not do is respond to Sampson's insult by drawing. What specifically might each of them be doing instead?

What do you imagine the "master's kinsman" doing as this fight begins? After all, it's for his benefit. How might he react to what he is seeing and hearing? Could he encourage the fight? How? Could he try to stop it? How?

And what physical event could impel Sampson to say:

SAMPSON   (Continued)
                          . . . Gregory, remember thy
swashing blow.

Some editions refer to this command as a call for a "washing blow," a kind of sword stroke effective against bucklers, or small shields. Taken literally, this could mean that Abraham and Balthasar are wearing shields. If so, that should take you back to the original question at the time of their entrance: What would two men wearing shields have come here to do? Will we see them do it?

Or could Sampson be calling on Gregory to fight more effectively, to remember a technique he seems to have forgotten? The meaning of the line will become clear once you have decided what Abraham and Balthasar—and what Gregory and the Capulet kinsman and everyone else you have placed in view—do just before the line.

(They fight.)

How do they fight? What, specifically, could be the way each fighter handles his weapons? Imagine each physical move of the fight; picture each blow and riposte as you would the lines of a scene—as an act that is a response to an act, and as an act that has specific physical consequences.

What consequences could this fight have for those who are not directly involved?

BENVOLIO
Part, fools! put up thy swords; you know not what you do.

Where did Benvolio come from, do you suppose? And when did he arrive? Some editions of the text indicate his entrance with a stage direction just before Gregory's line, "here comes one of my master's kinsmen." But Benvolio is Romeo's cousin—a Montague, not a Capulet. So the line cannot refer to him. Imagine a specific entrance for Benvolio.

What might Benvolio be doing, physically, before the fighting interrupts him and makes him try to break up the brawl?

Shakespeare has written a chopped up line: "Part fools! / put up thy swords; / you know not what you do." What might happen between each phrase? What events might drive Benvolio deeper and deeper into the middle of the fight?

(Beats down their swords.)

Does he? Only some editions include directions that claim Benvolio "beats down" anything. Do you imagine that the best—most engaging—completion of this story calls for Benvolio to succeed in breaking up the fight, at least momentarily, at this point? Do you have another idea to try out?

If Benvolio does have this moment of success, how specifically could he achieve it? If not, what happens instead? And how could that be the stimulus that logically causes the next event?:

TYBALT

What, art thou drawn among these heartless hinds?
Turn thee, Benvolio, look upon thy death.

Do you imagine that Tybalt was there, just waiting for the chance to jump in? What could he have been doing while he was waiting for his chance? Or did he act to create his opportunity? How?

Benvolio has drawn his sword. (When? What occurrence might have led to that event?) What's the most interesting way you can find for Tybalt to use his weapon plausibly against Benvolio?

If you chose to imagine this scene as a public event, what will each of these Citizens do next? After all, the fight has now escalated from a fight between servants to a death threat between principal members of each family. How might the citizenry behave, individually, when they hear Tybalt's challenge?

BENVOLIO

I do but keep the peace. Put up thy sword
Or manage it to part these men and me.

What might have happened in the original fight by this time? Why does Benvolio seem to need the help he's calling for? Could Tybalt's threat have caused it to flare up again? Might it have begun to spread (by accident or intention?) to involve the Citizens witnessing the brawl?

TYBALT

What, drawn, and talk of peace! I hate the word
As I hate hell, all Montagues, and thee:
Have at thee, coward.

Picture this fight in specific active detail. Might we have two fights now, one continuing between the servants, and a second between the cousins? How is each individual fighting, or trying to avoid the fight? What is the specific progression of blows, parries, chases, accidents, wounds, and escapes you can imagine?

(When Franco Zeffirelli staged the scene, he placed the fight in the middle of a crowded street market with striking results, as the fight between a few led to accidents and inflamed tempers that reduced the whole market into a shambles of overturned stalls, spilled goods of all sorts, wounded brawlers, innocent victims. In Michael Bagdanov's modern setting for the play, he staged the fight with knives and motor bikes in the city square. In each case, a distinct chain reaction of comic and frightening incidents was imagined that showed a unique civil chaos that the family feud could lead to.)

As you arrange incidents in your imagination, make them lead plausibly to the next thing that comes about:

> *Enter several of both Houses, who join*
> *the fray; then enter* CITIZENS *with clubs.*

Again, an ambiguous stage direction. Other editions propose other weapons ("partisans") or other characters ("An Officer"). Your job is to transform the general sense of a spreading riot suggested by these varied directions into a completed visible action by improvising each specific event that might plausibly occur and choosing the most persuasive sequence of acts to bring to the stage.

Which characters will you choose to appear? Where might they come from? Members of each house could come from each house. Could they also come from other places? Citizens could come from their own places of work. Where are they? If there's an Officer, what brings him here, and from where? What might he do, if you imagine a single policeman facing a spreading riot? What results might his act bring about?

1 CITIZEN

Clubs, bills, and partisans! Strike! Beat them down! Down with the Capulets! Down with the Montagues!

Does one person say all these contradictory things? Are the phrases of this speech more plausibly spoken by different people? Which ones? To whom? In response to what specific incident in each case? What reaction could each cry evoke?

"Bills" and "partisans" are large weapons, used for crowd control in the cities and for unhorsing armored knights in field combat. They are made of hooked and sharpened iron blades mounted at the end of long poles. You might think that the wielding of these weapons in a confined and crowded space already containing a couple of sword fights (at least) would have specific consequences. What might they be?

There are at least three camps in this city—the Capulets, the Montagues, and the Prince's family (which includes Mercutio and the County Paris)—who have an interest in the public peace. Do your citizens choose sides as the fighting spreads? What could each of them do within the melee as a result of their allegiances?

Not everybody has swords, clubs, bills, or partisans, perhaps. What else could individuals find in this place to fight, or protect themselves, with? Paving stones? Vegetables? Fish? Furniture?

Enter CAPULET *in his gown, and* LADY CAPULET.

CAPULET

What noise is this?

What gown? Has he been raised from his bed? (Benvolio will soon say that he has been out early searching for Romeo, who didn't come home last night.) Or is this a gown of office? How, specifically, will his clothing affect his behavior and the behavior of those who notice him?

What noise? By this time, there are plenty of noises to choose from. Can you imagine one particular one that brings Capulet out? Who could make it? How? What event might cause it to happen?

What will you have Capulet discover as he enters? What is the specific event that could cause him to call:

CAPULET   (Continued)
—Give me my long sword, ho!

A long sword, a massive, two handled weapon designed for use between fully armored warriors, seems a peculiar choice for a man to call for while he's wearing his gown. What could have happened that might plausibly drive him to choose such an impractical, ceremonial weapon?

To whom might he be shouting? To Lady Capulet? To a servant? To someone in the fight? What response could he get?

We know the words of the response he gets from his wife:

LADY CAPULET
A crutch! A crutch!

But to whom, specifically, are these words directed? Could she be literally calling for a crutch to help support her husband? What might she see happen that could lead her to call for crutches? Or could she be sarcastically deflating her husband's pretensions as a fighter by publicly trying to embarrass him out of taking part in the fight? What act would accomplish that?

What specific physical response could she get? From whom? How might that response cause her to say:

LADY CAPULET   (Continued)
. . . Why call you for a sword?

CAPULET
My sword I say!

Again, choose a person for Capulet to order about. If it is Lady Capulet, the action of the scene will be quite different than if you choose to explore the possibilities of a moment that shows a servant caught between the conflicting commands of his master and his mistress.

Do you imagine that Capulet is explaining his reasons to his wife, or perhaps discovering something new when he says:

CAPULET
—Old Montague is come,
And flourishes his blade in spite of me.

When, exactly, might Old Montague appear? When, and how, could he have armed himself?

Do you imagine him "flourishing" his blade, or might that only be Capulet's interpretation of what he is seeing? What might Old Montague be doing instead?

Where is this exchange between the two masters taking place? How could it plausibly happen with all the rest of the riot under way? And what, specifically, might be going on in that battle at this point?

What could Lady Capulet do in response to Capulet's pointing out Old Montague? What will you have her do next?

MONTAGUE

Thou villain Capulet!

What might happen that could make Montague call Capulet names at this particular moment?

What is the effect that the appearance of the two masters of the warring houses might have on the participants in the original brawl? How will the match of insults between Capulet and Montague appear to change the behavior of everyone who sees and hears it?

MONTAGUE   (Continued)
—Hold me not, let me go.

LADY MONTAGUE

Thou shalt not stir a foot to seek a foe.

Now both heads of the households, men of importance and worth, are part of the fight—and both of them have their wives restraining them in public. Will you have them behave "both alike in dignity" at this moment? What, physically, will each of them do? How, specifically, will you have each of the wives respond? And how might their behavior provoke specific acts to further inflame the situation into the chaos the Prince faces as he enters:

Enter PRINCE, *with* ATTENDANTS.

From where could the Prince enter? Does the brawl call him out? Could he discover it on his way to another place?

Who could these "attendants" be? Are they men at arms, specifically brought to put down the fighting? Could these people be members of his court, a court whose civil business is infuriatingly disrupted by this pointless violence? Are the attendants armed and ready to act, or could they be people who have to respond to what they find without recourse to weaponry? What can you imagine this train of attendants doing as they enter the scene of the riot?

PRINCE

Rebellious subjects, enemies to peace,
Profaners of this neighbor-stained steel,—
Will they not hear?

The Prince cannot even finish his sentence. What might each of the people in the scene be doing *instead* of listening to the Prince? You know that people have been stabbed ("neighbor-stained steel"), but you don't yet know what each stabbing has caused to happen next. The reaction to a stabbing could be extraordinary; at any rate, it's strong enough to drown out the Prince and the specific activities of each of his attendants. Imagine the visible steps in that story.

What will the Attendants do next? Could they be the ones whose action gives the Prince the confidence to try again? What action could make the Prince plausibly choose this moment to say:

> PRINCE   (Continued)
> 　　　　—What, ho! you men, you beasts,
> That quench the fire of your pernicious rage
> With purple fountains issuing for your veins,—

And then the subject suddenly changes. Might there be a development in the riot that causes the Prince to move on to his next threat, the decree of torture? What can you think might have happened at that moment to drive the Prince to say:

> PRINCE   (Continued)
> On pain of torture, from these bloody hands
> Throw your mistemper'd weapons to the ground,
> And hear the sentence of your moved prince.—

Do they throw their weapons down? What might happen to those weapons, specifically? What might happen to Sampson's "tool" and Benvolio's sword? Who could end up with Capulet's "Long Sword" and Montague's "brandished blade?" Who gets all those "bills, clubs, and partisans?" How, specifically, could this riot be quelled?

How will each brawler surrender? Might some of them imagine they have won something? Might some of them be swearing to finish the business the Prince has interrupted? Might some of them try to escape? Which ones? When?

What will the Prince be doing while the rioters are disarmed? Is he part of that action? Could he be trying to decide how to respond? Might he choose to look for evidence to determine who is at fault? At what moment might he conceive of his sentence?:

> PRINCE
> Three civil brawls, bred of an airy word,
> By thee, old Capulet and Montague,
> Have thrice disturb'd the quiet of our streets;

Literally speaking, this is incorrect. The "airy word" was neither Old Capulet's nor Montague's; it was Sampson's. What physical act might the Prince have witnessed that could have led him to conclude that the specific instigators of this fight were the heads of each household? And how would each character respond to a version of the scene that they know to be, in literal terms at least, a false accusation?

Or if you choose another dramatic meaning for the Prince's analysis of the outrage, what visible event might plausibly lead him to choose to blame the old men for the behavior of their servants and charges?

What physical relationship between the Prince and the fathers can you imagine for this moment? Could the Prince have had them arrested? Are they standing before him? If so, how might they behave toward each other? If not, where else might you place them? How would those locations suggest the way they are behaving as the Prince pronounces his sentence?

How might the Citizens, each of them, respond to the sight of these important arrests?

PRINCE   (Continued)
And made Verona's ancient citizens
Cast by their grave beseeming ornaments
To wield old partisans in hands as old,
Canker'd with peace, to part your canker'd hate:

How might each character accept, or physically reject, the Prince's analysis of the situation? What might Tybalt be doing, for example? Or Lady Capulet? Or a Citizen whose source of income was destroyed in the chaos? Or Sampson, who might be aware that he had started it all?

PRINCE   (Continued)
If ever you disturb our streets again,
Your lives shall pay the forfeit of the peace.

How might each character respond to this decision? What does each person physically do upon hearing that one more fight means that both Old Capulet and Old Montague will he executed by the state? That's big news. An audience will come to understand how important that news is by watching the physical reactions it causes in each of the characters who hear it.

PRINCE   (Continued)
For this time, all the rest depart away:—

Do they? Whom will you have leave, and who stay? How, physically could those who leave do it? As if they were escaping? To go to find a doctor? To hide from their masters? How will those you choose to have stay do so? Stay to overhear what happens next? Stay to clean up? Stay because they are too hurt to move? Stay to try to continue the fight?

Could there be action in the crowd's responses to the Prince's order to disperse that leads him to decide to investigate further? Could there be a hesitation the Prince must satisfy, as he says:

PRINCE   (Continued)
You, Capulet, shall go along with me;—
And Montague, come you this afternoon
To know our further pleasure in this case
To old Freetown, our common judgment place.

How will you have Capulet and Montague react to this summons? What might the Prince mean when he decides to hold his hearings in "Freetown, our common judgment place?" We'll see a meaning when you choose a physical reaction to that phrase. Could he, for example, be assuring the crowd of Citizens that even Capulets and Montagues will be given common treatment before his court—that this riot has stripped them of all privilege in his eyes? How might that idea, or another dramatic meaning behind the speech, be made evident through the specific physical responses it appears to provoke?

PRINCE
Once more, on pain of death, all men depart.

And, with the exception of the Montagues who are engaged in the next scene, they all do. How? To where? In what order? What might the specific story of the aftermath of the riot be?

How might those specific ways of leaving help the audience account for things to follow: Romeo's discovery of the fight? Tybalt's threats at the party? Capulet's plans for the future of his family?

You've just gone through a lot of questions. And, if you've joined in on the process and imagined a series of specific answers to them, more questions must have occurred to you as you read.

But we cannot use everything that comes to mind, even if it is both logical and intriguing. A necessary part of an actor's reading, part of any working theatre artist's reading, is choosing. So many plausible and exciting theatrical possibilities can occur to you as you read these texts, it's easy to lose the broad outlines of a story in the fascinating complexity of the details of moment-to-moment behavior.

So choose. Select one clean line of physical action. Choose acts that are specific and defined by their causes and their consequences. Then connect each act so that Mamet's "syllogism" becomes, "If A, then B; if B, then C; if C, then . . ."

A persuasive story should begin to emerge.

CHAPTER 6

Given Circumstances

One of the things that fascinated me about the part was that I was actually going to walk on stage holding somebody's head, and that seemed to me a tremendous challenge, something I looked forward to very much.—And also to wipe blood all over somebody's face. Those are the things that excite you about a part. I mean, they seem so melodramatic that you say to yourself, "Well, how can you possibly get away with that, make it believable," and you want to try.[22]
—Peggy Ashcroft

Peggy Ashcroft is talking about her preparation to play Margaret of Anjou in Peter Hall's production of *The Wars of the Roses*. The head she speaks of is the head of Margaret's lover and political ally, Suffolk. The blood is the blood of Rutland, soaking a handkerchief, and the "somebody's face" her character will smear blood on belongs to Rutland's father, the Duke of York. Speaking of melodrama, the next thing Margaret will do is grab a knife, and, in a spasm of fury, repeatedly stab the weeping father to death.

The actress was wisely cautious as she approached this extravagant incident. The straightforward logic of a chain of physical action provoking subsequent physical events might not be enough to sustain the audience's belief in such a gory illusion.

But the physical acts and utterances that make up a play should not appear to stand alone. An essential part of the dramatic illusion is

70

that these incidents seem to exist in a context, a context made of all those fictional conditions in the story actors call "the given circumstances."

The appearance of circumstances influencing an act can go a long way toward making even the most extreme action seem plausible in the theatre. Margaret of Anjou is a character whose story is carefully developed over four of Shakespeare's texts. If the spectators can be led to understand the forces that might be at work in Margaret's *mind* from this long and complex background, and to grant that those particular conditions might well drive someone to act in this extraordinary way, perhaps they can make the leap of faith that makes the theatrical moment terrifying. Achieving this connection between given circumstances and action is the next step in the process of improvising an illusion for the stage.

So, once you've begun to picture a chain of physical action for a scene, read again. Try to discover all the conditions that might be at work behind your chosen actions and reactions. To get you started, here are four kinds of given circumstances to consider:

1. In plays you can read ahead. Some of the events in the future of the play will appear to be directly and logically conditioned by the behavior you are imagining for the present scene. Read ahead, then look back. What can you discover and imagine from the rest of the text that might lead you back to specific improvisations for this moment? How can the incidents the audience will see next suggest things to you about the particular nature of the acts you are improvising for the scene at hand?

2. In real life, people have a past that affects the way they behave in the present. To be convincing as fictional people, characters, too, need to appear to be speaking and acting in response to a personal history. So, as you read, begin to imagine a history of events and sensations for each character, consistent with (and never distracting from) the information given in the text, a history that could lead to a specific completion of the action for this scene.

3. Ask, for each moment of action, what is at stake for the character? What could that character win or lose as a result of each act and utterance they make? What specific risk is each character running as he or she behaves in a particular way? The thing that is at stake for the characters as they act will suggest ideas about how they act.

4. If you want to test the effects the circumstances of place and

time have on behavior, try this little experiment: Imagine saying the words, "Damn it, where did I put my keys?" How might you behave if you spoke them a) late for work in your apartment amid the leavings of a party the night before?; b) standing up in a crowded church just after Easter services?; c) crawling around under a park bench at 3:00 in the morning with a policeman near by?; d) late for class, standing naked before a locked locker in a gymnasium; or e) in a dark and shadowy parking garage? The words are the same in each situation, but the physical properties of the place and the pressures of time make everything else that might happen distinct.

So, as you imagine the action of a scene in a play, ask: What is the physical environment in which that action occurs? Where does this happen? How can each event of the scene fit into the architecture of this room? What is the virtual function of this space; that is, do you want to imagine the action of a scene in a cathedral? Or a swimming pool? Or a bookstore? Who is in this place at this time? What influence does each character bring to bear on the other characters' action as they inhabit this space together?

Go on to imagine the effects of time on this space: What time of day will you choose? Of year? Of historical period? How much time might each character believe there is to accomplish what he or she wants to do here? How might each of these considerations of time determine the particular behavior you'll choose for the scene?

That's a lot of given circumstances to look for. Finding and revealing such a detailed context for Margaret of Anjou's bloodcurdling moments of action must have been a vital part of the "tremendous challenge" facing Peggy Ashcroft as she looked forward to rehearsing and performing her role.

Hamlet and Ophelia don't act as extravagantly as Queen Margaret, but their "nunnery scene," too, is a passage that, taken by itself, can appear overcharged, repetitive, and melodramatic. It's another moment that vividly illustrates a challenge facing the actor in any scene: to convince an audience by choosing a sharply defined context of given circumstances for the conflict they are about to watch:

HAMLET
—Soft you now!
The Fair Ophelia.—Nymph, in thy orisons
Be all my sins remembered.

OPHELIA

Good my lord,
How does your honour for this many a day?

HAMLET

I humbly thank you; well, well, well.

OPHELIA

My lord, I have remembrances of yours,
That I have longed long to re-deliver;
I pray you, now receive them.

HAMLET

No, not I;
I never gave you aught.

OPHELIA

My honour'd lord, you know right well you did;
And, with them, words of so sweet breath composed
As made the things more rich: their perfume lost,
Take these again; for to the noble mind
Rich gifts wax poor when givers prove unkind.
There, my lord.

HAMLET

Ha, ha! are you honest?

OPHELIA

My lord?

HAMLET

Are you fair?

OPHELIA

What means your lordship?

HAMLET

That if you be honest and fair, your honesty should admit no
discourse to your beauty.

OPHELIA

Could beauty, my lord, have better commerce than with
honesty?

HAMLET

Ay, truly; for the power of beauty will sooner transform
honesty from what it is to a bawd than the force of honesty
can translate beauty into his likeness: this was sometime a
paradox, but now the time gives it proof. I did love you
once.

OPHELIA

Indeed, my lord, you made me believe so.

HAMLET

You should not have believed me; for virtue cannot so
inoculate our old stock but we shall relish of it: I loved
you not.

OPHELIA

I was the more deceived.

HAMLET

Get thee to a nunnery: why wouldst thou be a breeder of
sinners? I am myself indifferent honest; but yet I could
accuse me of such things that it were better my mother had
not born me: I am very proud, revengeful, ambitious; with
more offenses at my beck than I have thoughts to put them
in, imagination to give them shape, or time to act them in.
What should such fellows as I do crawling between heaven and
earth? We are arrant knaves, all; believe none of us. Go
thy ways to a nunnery. Where's your father?

OPHELIA

At home, my lord.

HAMLET

Let the doors be shut upon him, that he may play the fool
nowhere but in's own house. Farewell.

OPHELIA

O, help him, you sweet heavens!

HAMLET

If thou dost marry, I'll give thee this plague for thy
dowry,—be thou as chaste as ice, as pure as snow, thou
shalt not escape calumny. Get thee to a nunnery, go:

farewell. Or, if thou needs marry, marry a fool; for wise
men know well enough what monsters you make of them. To a
nunnery, go; and quickly too. Farewell.

OPHELIA

O heavenly powers, restore him!

HAMLET

I have heard of your paintings too, well enough; God has
given you one face and you make yourselves another; you jig,
you amble, and you lisp, and nickname God's creatures, and
make your wantonness your ignorance. Go to, I'll no more on
it; it hath made me mad. I say, we will have no more
marriages: those that are married already, all but one,
shall live; the rest shall keep as they are. To a nunnery,
go.

(Exit.)

OPHELIA

O, what a noble mind is here o'erthrown!
The courtier's, soldier's, scholar's eye, tongue, sword:
The expectancy and rose of the fair state,
The glass of fashion and the mould of form,
The observ'd of all observers,—quite, quite down!
And I, of ladies most deject and wretched
That suck'd the honey of his music vows,
Now see that noble and most sovereign reason,
Like sweet bells jangled, out of tune and harsh:
That unmatch'd form and feature of blown youth
Blasted with ecstasy: O, woe is me,
To have seen what I have seen, see what I see!

(*Re-enter* KING *and* POLONIUS.)

Read closely and you'll find that the text is full of suggestive in-
dications about the circumstances at work. Some elements in the situations are explicit, specifically detailed in the language of this or
other scenes in the play. But, once again, the text is incomplete. Other
given circumstances at work in the situation remain implicit only,
waiting for actors, directors, and designers to ask questions and make
specific choices consistent with the text. Once the issue of given cir-

cumstances comes up, a reader has a great deal of improvisation ahead.

The first kind of given circumstance listed above was the consequences of each act, and how that dramatic future might suggest ideas to you about the present action as you read. Begin by reading this scene with that future in mind.

The text spells out explicit consequences of the nunnery scene: When Hamlet next appears, he is instructing the players and commenting on the nature of acting. It's useful advice that he gives, but one striking thing about it is that there is no mention of Ophelia or the events of the previous scene at all. It seems as if the action of the scene with the players, the set up of the "mousetrap" to catch the conscience of the king, and the protestation of friendship to Horatio could all have occurred exactly as they do whether or not Hamlet had dismissed Ophelia. With the possible exception of Hamlet's mention of an admiration for men who are not "passion's slave," it's as if the nunnery scene never happened. But it did.

Claudius (remember that Claudius and Polonius, although they have no words to say, are active elements of the nunnery scene and must always be kept in mind) will come out of hiding and reject Polonius's diagnosis of Hamlet's apparent instability. He will sense danger in Hamlet's presence, and then he will announce his decision to send him immediately to England. The audience will soon discover that Claudius, by choosing England, means to send Hamlet to his death.

Polonius will agree with the king's decision, but will go on to assert that his understanding of Hamlet's behavior is still the right one. He will then propose a delay, allowing time for a second spying session in the queen's closet. This proposal will cost the old man his life.

Perhaps the most evocative consequences of this scene are to be found in following Ophelia's story. The next time she appears she is in the midst of the gathered court, part of the audience for the play-within-the-play. Hamlet humiliates her with raw references to her sexuality for all the court to hear. After that, she appears mad, singing what seems to the court to be bawdy nonsense. Then we hear she has drowned. A mad girl's accident? A suicide? At any rate, the nunnery scene is the last time the audience will see her before she becomes an object of public abuse, madness, and death.

As you read the scene, ask what these consequences of the action suggest about the action of the scene itself. For example, what does the fact that Hamlet can act as if the nunnery scene had had no effect on him suggest to you? The violence of his language seems to indicate that the nunnery scene is a crucial episode to him. Later, he will swear that he loved Ophelia more than forty thousand brothers could. Yet he is able to offer a discourse on the aesthetics of the theatre immediately after berating the woman he says he loves. What specific *ways* of receiving and attacking Ophelia might make his apparent ability to put this scene aside seem likely?

What acts in the scene might cause Claudius to think that Hamlet's condition, once it is out in the open, "Will be some danger?" How could Claudius's decision to send Hamlet "with speed" to England grow out of what he, and the audience, will see in Hamlet's behavior?

By the same token, what acts could have led Polonius to disagree? What could he have seen happen between Ophelia and Hamlet that would lead him to urge the king to hold off for a short while to see if Gertrude can come up with a clearer explanation for the Prince's violent behavior?

What could you imagine happening in this scene that could account for Ophelia's dismal future? What detailed understandings of the events and speeches of this scene would plausibly lead to the specific forms of humiliation, insanity, and death she is about to face? Why is Hamlet's choice of public abuse of her in Act III, Scene ii articulated in terms of "country matters?" Look at the lyrics of her mad scenes—why might she choose those words? Could they suggest ideas for the way people might behave in the nunnery scene? And what about the story of the nunnery scene could plausibly lead to a suicide?

Now, read the scene again, looking for the second sort of given circumstance. Ask questions about personal histories for the characters that might account for the behavior indicated in the text and that might suggest specific ways of completing that behavior in physical terms. See what each character's possible past could suggest about the present you are trying to improvise.

First, find those elements of each character's past that are explicitly revealed in the text: Hamlet is a young man of intelligence and energy, of legal age to assume the crown of Denmark on his father's death, who returned from university for his father's funeral to discover that his uncle had assumed the throne and married his mother. He found that the court has agreed to this irregular assumption of power, and that, together, the new king and his court celebrate his ascension with drinking parties. Hamlet's mother has set aside her mourning for his father, publicly urged him to do the same, and appears to him to be a happy and enthusiastic bride in her new marriage; the prince finds this enthusiasm repugnant.

Hamlet, as the displaced legitimate heir, had allowed himself only one small act of defiance at first: he wore public mourning for his father after the official period of mourning ended. To placate him, Claudius made Hamlet his heir to the throne. Hamlet refused to be pacified. Then, seeking out the Ghost of his father, Hamlet learned that his suspicions were well founded; this new regime was the result of murder, seduction, and usurpation. He then swore to punish the guilty.

To do so, Hamlet launched a campaign of ridicule and enigmatic humor, defying the king, teasing courtiers, and testing friends from college who were sent to spy on him. This eccentric behavior in the heir apparent confused the court. They wondered whether the prince was losing his mind for love (Polonius has ordered Ophelia to send him away) or for policy. In either case, he became a danger to the existing government. He must be dealt with.

More immediately, Hamlet has just spoken two soliloquies: "O, what a rogue and peasant slave am I" and "To be, or not to be," the first filled with words of self-loathing, and the second, musing on suicide. This second has been overheard by his mortal enemies, Claudius and Polonius.

Claudius has chosen to establish his new reign with a foreign adventure, the war with Poland. He cannot fight a war abroad with a divided court at home. Hamlet is not cooperating. Why has Hamlet been acting so strangely, wearing nighted black, putting on an antic disposition, speaking in veiled threats to anyone who'll listen? What does he know? How did he find out? If Hamlet is truly mad, he will not be a threat because he can be put away as a mental incompetent. But if there is method in his madness, then Hamlet is a direct threat to Claudius's personal and political ambitions.

In the text, Polonius has been occupied up until now with familial decisions. He has decided to allow his son to go off to college, and won royal permission for this plan. He has sent Laertes off to Paris with good wishes and sage advice. He has also hired a man to follow his son and report back on the boy's private life. He has ordered his daughter to break off her relationship with Hamlet, and he has promised the king that he will solve the mystery of Hamlet's erratic behavior in the court.

What's Ophelia's explicit history? She and Hamlet have had a romantic relationship, and her father and brother both have warned her against relying on Hamlet's faith in the future. She has teased her brother about this, saying he had better practice what he preaches. Her father has forbidden her to see or hear a word from Hamlet. Princes who have just been named heirs to the throne cannot marry as they choose.

Later, she comes to her father to report a strange meeting in her room between her and Hamlet where she says he suddenly appeared with his clothes in disarray and wandered about like a man in what she agrees could have been "the very ecstasy of love."

Immediately before her confrontation with Hamlet, the text shows her being instructed by the King, the Queen, and Polonius. She is to pretend to come across Hamlet on her way to prayers. She is to play the role of returning love letters to him so that the King and Polonius ("lawful espials") can reach their decision: to treat Hamlet's affliction as harmless disappointment in love, or as a threat to the crown. She knows what she is about to do. She knows who is watching.

All these explicit circumstances at work in the scene suggest further questions for you to ask about those parts of each character's personal history that the text does *not* spell out.

For example, one constant speculation about these characters' personal histories is wondering whether or not Hamlet and Ophelia are lovers in the physical sense. Have Hamlet and Ophelia ever made love? (William Redfield's answer? "It's up to you, darling!"[23]) What could be the specific story of their relationship?

The reason this circumstance raises so much interest among actors is that it is a circumstance that could directly affect the way each character plays the action in this scene. If they are lovers, two young people who have defied their elders to express their love physically, they would, in all likelihood, behave accordingly. How might this circumstance make Ophelia behave, knowing, as she does, that her father is listening? How might Hamlet use this circumstance as he berates Ophelia for her personal habits? Would this circumstance determine what each character means and understands when they talk about Hamlet's "sins"? Or about going to a "nunnery"? Specifically, how?

This scene is one of only two times when the audience will see Ophelia and Hamlet speaking together. But they have heard about a third time, a meeting that took place before this scene. In the first scene of the second act, Shakespeare has Ophelia come to her father:

Enter OPHELIA

POLONIUS
How now, Ophelia! what's the matter?

OPHELIA
Alas, my lord, I have been so affrighted!

POLONIUS
With what, i' the name of God?

OPHELIA
My Lord, as I was sewing in my chamber,
Lord Hamlet,—with his doublet all unbrac'd;
No hat upon his head; his stockings foul'd
Ungarter'd and down gyved to his ankle;
Pale as his shirt; his knees knocking each other;
And with a look so piteous in purport
As if he had been loosed out of hell
To speak of horrors,—he comes before me.

POLONIUS
Mad for thy love?

OPHELIA
My lord, I do not know;
But truly I do fear it.

POLONIUS
What said he?

OPHELIA

He took me by the wrist, and held me hard;
Then goes he to the length of all his arm;
And with the other hand, thus o'er his brow,
He falls to such perusal of my face
As he would draw it. Long stay'd he so;
At last,—a little shaking of my arm,
And thrice his head thus waving up and down,—
He rais'd a sigh so piteous and profound
That it did seem to shatter all his bulk
And end his being: that done, he lets me go
And, with his head over his shoulder turn'd,
He seem'd to find his way without his eyes;
For out o' doors he went without their help,
And to the last bended their light on me.

What might have really happened in this off-stage encounter? One way to imagine it is literally. Ophelia could be simply reporting exactly what happened in her story. In his film version of the play, Laurence Olivier made that choice, enacting this moment in flashback as Jean Simmons spoke the lines as a voice-over. But is that the only possibility available to you?

Look at the given circumstances influencing this off-stage scene:

1. Ophelia is reporting this incident to her father, the person who has absolute authority over her and who has ordered her, because of her political position at court, never to "give words or talk with the Lord Hamlet."

2. Ophelia has said that Hamlet is a man whose professions of love she has believed. (And whose love she may have accepted and consummated?)

3. Polonius is sometimes dismissed as a wordy fool. Well, perhaps. That certainly is one choice with a long and popular stage tradition. But if that were all he was, you might wonder why Claudius would be likely to choose him as his right-hand man. Would your Claudius trust a man who had no more to offer than aphorisms? Could it have been Polonius whose political calculations within the court allowed Claudius to ascend the throne on the death of old Hamlet, usurping it from a perfectly qualified prince? What might happen if his international ambitions mirror those of Claudius? His name,

"Polonius," could suggest that, like "Coriolanus," he preferred to be called by a title celebrating a military victory rather than by a common name. And, in this case, the victory would have been over the Poles. It's certainly plausible to choose a Polonius other than the conventional one, the dodderer who is full of art and empty of matter. It's possible to read the text and imagine a man with a personal history of important political manipulations, the man of power fully capable of using that power effectively and mercilessly to achieve the political ends he wants. Could Ophelia know something of her father's political history?

4. Your Polonius could be a man with complex fears and ambitions for his family as well as for the policy of his government. What might result if you chose to imagine a Polonius who needs to manipulate his children so that they live publicly spotless lives? It's a plausible choice. The audience has just seen that he is not above sending people to spy on his own children; he's just ordered Reynaldo to go to Paris and libel his son in order to try to pry information loose about Laertes' personal life. Couldn't your Ophelia be aware of her father's hopes and his way of imposing those hopes on the privacy of his family? She comes in at the end of the Reynaldo scene; couldn't she know that her father uses spies on his children?

Given these circumstances, what might happen if, in the off-stage scene, Hamlet had come to his lover's bedroom for affection and solace in his moment of crisis after the confrontation with the Ghost? Perhaps one possibility could be that Ophelia would be afraid that one of her father's spies would report the prince's arrival to her father, revealing everything illicit that had gone on secretly between the lovers.

To protect the secret of a love affair, can you imagine an Ophelia who might have run away from Hamlet and taken the risk of trying to reach her father before the supposed spy could report the truth? Perhaps she could feel she had to give the old man an innocent story (a lie) that would explain away the appearance of the Prince in her room with his clothes in disarray. Might that not suggest at least one interesting new Ophelia capable of a wide range of complex and assertive behaviors as the play unfolds? (As Director Robin Phillips noted when he was working on the play for the Stratford Festival, "I have a dread of those pixie Ophelias . . ."[24])

Now, in light of this understanding of the off-stage scene Ophelia has reported to Polonius, go back to the scene at hand: How might Hamlet judge Ophelia's thinking in the "nunnery scene" if he were acting in response to a previous scene where his search for comfort in her arms drove her to go and make a report to his enemy, her father? How might she assess her situation if she were trying to keep her previous lie intact, knowing, as she does, that her father is spying on the lovers' confrontation? In other words, what might be at stake for each character? How might each of their perceptions of the possible gains or losses they risk in this situation impel them to act, in specific terms, as the scene unfolds? Make some choices about your characters' stakes in the outcome of this moment of conflict. Come up with physical action that could result from this background to the scene.

Now try again. Find different risks for each character to run and see what alternative ideas for action arise. Look for what else might be at stake.

To start your imagination going in a new direction, here's another improvisation for the given circumstances of the scene to think about. Frances Barber is exchanging early thoughts about the role in rehearsal with her director:

> On first discussing the part with the director, Ron Daniels, I excitedly told him of my discoveries:
> "She's full of humor and wit and intelligence, she's strong, courageous, emotionally open. She shows her independence when she gives Hamlet his 'remembrances' back, she stands up to her father, she . . ."
> "Frankie, you *can't* play her as a feminist, it's not in the text."
> "Oh but it is, Ron, oh but it is." (I had done my justification research rather thoroughly.)
> "Why does she go mad then?"
> "Because she's the only person in the play who sees what's going on."
> "And?"
> "And she's full of guilt for not having been able to prevent it."
> "And?"
> "And she's full of remorse for her father's death."
> "And?"
> "And she blames herself for Hamlet's prejudice against women."
> "And?"

"And she's guilt ridden, Ron! She's utterly guilt ridden, like every woman I know; and she's culpable to a point because she knew Claudius and Polonius were spying on Hamlet but she didn't warn him. And she knows he's physically attracted to her and she sort of encourages it."[25]

Frances Barber's early ideas suggest a very different sense of what could be at stake for her Ophelia. They suggest an Ophelia who might be trying, in the impossible circumstance of being closely watched, to warn Hamlet about the trap he's in. The greatest risk to Frances Barber's Ophelia is that she might fail because of Hamlet's complex feelings for her and the behavior those feelings generate—and she does.

This improvisation also suggests a particular risk at hand for Hamlet. Frances Barber goes on to report that Roger Rees chose to play a Hamlet who ran the risk of giving in to his sexual attraction for Ophelia. His prince did not appear to be driven by political fears or anger at betrayal as much as by an intense fear of his own personal vulnerabilities. He berated and abused Ophelia because his love for her was a threat to his own resolution, just as love for Gertrude had led to his father's downfall, and Gertrude's obvious sense of sexual fulfillment with Claudius opened the door to murder and usurpation. Driven by the given circumstance of these fears and desires, his Hamlet kissed Ophelia passionately, then, realizing what was at stake, heaped abuse on her, punishing her for the effect her beauty had on him. The result was an example of a new nunnery scene, a startling yet logical improvisation driven by the characters' apparent sense of what was at stake in the given moment.

Carry on: What are the risks your Polonius might be running as the scene progresses? What are his stakes in its outcome? Will your Polonius, as Claudius' chief minister, know of the debts England owes Denmark that Claudius calls on in Act IV, Scene iii? Could Polonius be aware of the mortal danger the prince and heir to the throne of Denmark faces in England? How might that awareness cause Polonius to behave as he hears the king's decision? Can you imagine a Polonius who has staked his reputation with the new king, or his ambitions for his daughter, or even, perhaps, his life ("take this from this," he says to the King and Queen, pointing to his head and shoulders, "if this be otherwise") on his diagnosis for Hamlet's odd behavior? How much might he have gambled on the idea that Hamlet is distracted because Ophelia has spurned him as he, her father, commanded her to do? What might Polonius believe will happen to him if the scene fails to go as he had predicted? (And it doesn't, does it?) How might those apprehensions make him behave as he emerges from his hiding place?

What might your Claudius be listening for? What's at stake for him? Could he be looking for an excuse to have Hamlet killed? Will he find it? Where? When? Who gives him that excuse? Claudius prepared Gertrude for this encounter, assuring her it was all for Hamlet's welfare. How could that promise impel Claudius's specific ways of spying? How might you imagine his ways of summing up what he has seen and heard? Were his predictions fulfilled? Justified? How could you tell that from the way he might behave?

The text doesn't offer us much direct information about the given circumstances of physical location or time for this scene, only—"A Room in the Castle." But you can find a good many indirect suggestions about the place when you explore the particular actions this room must plausibly accommodate. It must be a place in which the King and Queen could plausibly receive Rosencrantz and Guildenstern's first report on Hamlet's "affliction." It must be a place where Polonius and Claudius could set their trap, a place where they can find a convenient hiding place from which they can watch Hamlet and Ophelia as they meet, hearing every word. It must be a place where Hamlet could think himself alone, a place where he could feel safe enough to reveal his inner thoughts in the "To be, or not to be" soliloquy. And it must be a place where Hamlet could reasonably accept the notion that he had met Ophelia accidentally as she was on her way to prayers.

Imagine your own specific location for the scene in detail. Then go through the scene step by step looking for the likely effects that place might have on the character's behavior: Why might your choice for a place prompt Hamlet to reveal his secret fears? Where would the king and Polonius "bestow themselves?" How might your Hamlet reveal himself to Ophelia in these surroundings? How could Hamlet use the physical properties of the space to punish Ophelia? How might Ophelia use the room to protect herself, to respond to Hamlet's cruel remarks, or try to warn the prince?

A clearly chosen place may well help you determine your own answer to another long disputed moment in the scene: When, exactly, does Hamlet learn that he is being overheard? A customary solution is that his discovery of the fact is marked by the sharp change of subject in the text, Hamlet's sudden question, "where is thy father?" The notion is that something happens (choose: specifically what?) that reveals the spies to Hamlet, and he asks the question to test Ophelia's faith, a test she fails where she lies and tells Hamlet that Polonius is "at home." This obvious betrayal is often shown to set Hamlet off on his second round of abuse, punishing her for setting him up in front of his enemies.

But Peter Hall, directing the play with Albert Finney in the leading role, improvised a different solution:

> Tuesday, 7 October
> Important findings at rehearsal. Hamlet is not concerned that Rosencrantz and Guildernstern are spies; nor is he concerned in the Ophelia nunnery scene that he is being overheard. These scenes are not about these discoveries; he knows them in a flash. He's concerned about the honesty of the characters in their replies when he charges them with duplicity, and both scenes show him trying to demonstrate his philosophy, anxiously, vigorously. They are a pattern of misunderstandings.
>
> And when Albert walked on stage and launched into the current problem of Hamlet—was he to be or not to be?—it was electric and urgent, not introspective. I'm sure that's right.[26]

What's your solution? And whether Hamlet discovers the duplicity in a flash or learns it over the course of the action of the scene, how might this discovery be physically accomplished? What could the geography of the place, the architecture, the light, the furnishing, the entire and specific nature of this place and time suggest to you about steps in the story of your Hamlet's discovery?

There is, of course, an element of the chicken-and-the-egg in the process of reading to find specific and promising given circumstances for a scene. Imagining those specific circumstances that cast fresh light on the physical action you have chosen will suggest even more ideas for action, just as specific improvisations of what is literally going on will suggest more and more telling details about the context. Good. The object is neither to choose startling behavior for its own sake nor to reveal circumstances to an audience as if the invention of a novel background for each moment were an end in itself. The object is to continue to explore the possibilities offered by the text, finding persuasive connections between a detailed context and a specific physical action. Imaginative speculation about the logic at work *between* the given circumstances at work in a moment of action and the particular behavior those circumstances suggest for the stage can be among the most productive ways you can (in Peggy Ashcroft's words) "possibly get away with that, make it believable."

CHAPTER 7

Intentional Action

I don't think there's much doubt about it, is there? Playing the quality (of a character) leads to bad acting, and going for the intention is more interesting and alive and human.[27]

—JOHN BARTON

Try to recall some moments of striking behavior from your own experience. I can remember, for example, seeing a couple walking alone along a college path in the sunlight. Suddenly, the young woman of the pair dropped her books, threw her arms in the air, hugged herself, and danced in a tiny circle. Then she picked up her books and moved on. I can recall a teenager, dressed in a tinseled robe with large dark circles painted around his eyes, staring fixedly at me through a window as I sat in his parents' house. He licked the glass.

Watching, I was curious; I wanted to understand what I had seen. Behind each of these physical incidents, there were a lot of circumstances that were explicit to me, and I enjoyed the imagination game of adding to them when I had enough time and distance to make some likely guesses. But striking acts and circumstances by themselves weren't sufficient. The acts I had witnessed were on purpose; these people *chose* to act as they did. The questions I needed to ask were: "*Why* are you doing that? What can you be thinking? What do you expect will happen next as a result? What do you intend?"

Spectators at a play also are curious about the extraordinary events they are watching and want to understand them in the same way. Most of the action in a play represents behavior that is voluntary; so, most of the time, an audience needs the same sort of information I did if the illusion is going to succeed. Audiences need to see characters acting as if they could think for themselves and as if they had specific intentions in mind.

This means that, in addition to reading to discover a plausible chain reaction of visible events for the stage and a suggestive understanding of the context of a scene, an actor or a director needs to develop an imagination for acts that create the appearance of thought, an illusion of characters who are actively pursuing their own immediate and specific purposes. We need to improvize action that seems intentional.

There is a direct connection between the physical acts of a scene, the given circumstances both explicit and improvised for the moment, and the illusion of a character's intention. When you are imagining the given circumstances for a scene, look for elements in that situation that offer a problem, a dilemma, a desire, or a trap. Find a *status quo* in the circumstances each character cannot accept for one reason or another. Then look again at the physical action of the scene, including the acts of speaking.

What you'll discover is that each character can be understood as spending his or her time on stage trying to fix things. The literal behavior of a scene, each action and reaction the audience watches, can become understandable once it is revealed to be a character's specific attempt to *change* unsatisfactory circumstances.

So for each moment of action, a character should appear to have a particular change in the situation he or she wants to bring about—an intention (or, to use the argot of acting, "an objective"). Some of Shakespeare's characters (Richard III, perhaps) state their ambitions for change unambiguously, then act in a complex pattern of actions intended to fulfill them, inviting the audience to watch the process. Others (Iago comes to mind) have led actors on a merry chase of speculation and invention about what objectives might make them tick. In either case, you'll find that reading the text to imagine detailed physical action and circumstances can also suggest ideas about each character's likely intentions. At the same time, imagining specific and appropriate ideas for the immediate results each character might appear to expect, or hope for, as he or she acts can suggest new and engaging behaviors the actor might try. Discovering context and action can suggest intentions; improvising appropriate hopes and expectations can suggest ways of acting.

Hopes and expectations suggest another fundamental element in plays as well: conflict. In scenes with more than one character conflict arises when characters are seen to be working at cross purposes; one character's intended change in the situation can only be achieved at the expense of the accomplishment of another's hopes and purposes. Their objectives are irreconcilable.

In other words, dramatic conflict arises on stage when each character is working specifically in order to get another character to stop what he or she is doing, and to start doing a different particular thing that will fulfill the first character's intention. At the same time, the other character has a specific agenda, too. Conflicting characters resist each other's attempts make changes, and counter with acts intended to effect their own changes in the situation. So while one character may intend a speech or an act to produce one result, the other characters may understand, or make use of, what they are hearing or seeing in an entirely different way—responding to the first with an unexpected reaction, and pushing the conflict forward.

Try it. Here is a section of Act II, Scene ii of *A Midsummer Night's Dream.* How do you imagine Demetrius and Helena each intend to change their present situations? How might those conflicting desires lead them to do and say the particular things set down for them in the text?:

(*Enter* DEMETRIUS, HELENA *following him.*)

DEMETRIUS
I love thee not, therefore pursue me not.
Where is Lysander and fair Hermia?
The one I'll slay, the other slayeth me.
Thou told'st me they were stol'n unto this wood,
And here am I, and wood within this wood,
Because I cannot meet with Hermia.
Hence, get thee gone, and follow me no more.

HELENA

You draw me, you hard-hearted adamant;
But yet you draw not iron, for my heart
Is true as steel. Leave you your power to draw,
And I shall have no power to follow you.

DEMETRIUS

Do I entice you? Do I speak you fair?
Or, rather, do I not in plainest truth
Tell you I do not, nor I cannot love you?

HELENA

And even for that do I love you the more.
I am your spaniel; and, Demetrius,
The more you beat me, I will fawn on you:
Use me but as your spaniel, spurn me, strike me,
Neglect me, lose me; only give me leave,
Unworthy as I am, to follow you.
What worser place can I beg in your love,
And yet a place of high respect with me,—
Than to be used as you use your dog?

DEMETRIUS

Tempt not too much the hatred of my spirit;
For I am sick when I do look on thee.

DEMETRIUS

And I am sick when I look not on you.

DEMETRIUS

You do impeach your modesty too much,
To leave the city, and commit yourself
Into the hands of one that loves you not;
To trust the opportunity of night,
And the ill council of a desert place,
With the rich worth of your virginity.

HELENA

Your virtue is my privilege for that.
It is not night when I do see your face,
Therefore I think I am not in the night:
Not doth this wood lack worlds of company;

For you, in my respect, are all the world:
Then how can it be said I am alone
When all the world is there to look on me?

DEMETRIUS

I'll run from thee and hide me in the brakes,
And leave thee to the mercy of wild beasts.

HELENA

The wildest hath not such a heart as you.
Run when you will, the story shall be chang'd;
Apollo flies, and Daphne holds the chase;
The dove pursues the griffin; the mild hind
Makes speed to catch the tiger,—bootless speed,
When cowardice pursues and valor flies.

DEMETRIUS

I will not stay thy question; let me go:
Or, if thou follow me, do not believe
But I shall do thee mischief in the wood.

HELENA

Ay, in the temple, in the town, the field,
You do me mischief. Fie, Demetrius!
Your wrongs do set a scandal on my sex:
We cannot fight for love as men may do:
We should be woo'd, and were not made to woo.
I'll follow thee, and make a heaven of hell,
To die upon the hand I love so well.

(*Exeunt* DEMETRIUS *and* HELENA.)

To sort out this pattern of conflicting intentions in this scene,
begin by picturing the given circumstances. Helena was once courted
by Demetrius, fell in love with him, and was bitterly hurt when
Demetrius took it into his head, with Egeus's encouragement, to break
off his relationship with Helena and seek to marry her friend Hermia
(who has fallen in love with another young man, Lysander). Still,
Helena does not give up hope that she will, in the end, become
Demetrius's wife.

By Theseus's order, unless Hermia agrees to her father's wish,
give up Lysander and marry Demetrius in four day's time, he will

condemn her to a life of seclusion in a convent or to the execution her angry father has demanded. There is a deadline in effect.

To escape this dilemma, Hermia and Lysander have agreed to elope through a wood to his aunt's house, seven leagues away from the city and beyond Theseus's jurisdiction.

Helena and Hermia have been friends since childhood. They used to come to this wood together to play and share secrets. In fact, it is the girls' secret hideout (which Lysander once discovered by accident) that will serve as the meeting place for Hermia and Lysander as they elope. Helena knows this (Hermia has told her) and knows how to find this place, at least in the daylight.

Helena, desperately trying to win Demetrius's affection back, has betrayed her friend's secret plan and has offered to guide Demetrius to the secret meeting place. He does not know where it is.

The wood is inhabited by a tribe of fairies invisible, most of the time, to mortals. Oberon, their king, is in a sort of custody battle with his queen, Titania, over the orphaned son of one of her "votaries." Their rancor has disturbed the natural order of the forest; "the seasons alter," Titania says.

Titania has just refused to give the boy to Oberon once again, so he has sent Puck to find a flower that was struck by Cupid's arrow; the juices of this magic flower can make people fall hopelessly in love. He plans to use it to humiliate Titania as punishment.

Helena and Demetrius break into this scene, and Oberon spies on them.

The scene is set in a wood at night. Demetrius and Helena have come here from the light and safety of the city and the court.

As a result of what Oberon sees in this scene, he will decide to give Puck a piece of the magic flower to anoint Demetrius's eyes so that Helena will get the man she wants. This leads to Puck's mistake—daubing the charmed juice in the wrong lover's eyes—and to all the confusions and misdirected passions that make up the story of the foursome of young lovers.

This much is explicit in the text. Now, imagine your own completed picture of the situation by improvising those necessary circumstances missing from, but consistent with, the text. Here are some questions to get you started:

Imagine Demetrius and Helena's story in detail. How old do you imagine each to be? How experienced? Why, specifically, *did your*

Demetrius suddenly reject Helena for Hermia? How might each of them interpret that story? (A review of Helena's soliloquy at the end of Act I, Scene i might give you some ideas to start with.)

What could it be about Helena that Demetrius once loved and now says he detests? Could he still be vulnerable to Helena at the present moment? How? What specific reason could your Helena still have for continuing to "dote" on Demetrius? What saving quality could she remember from their happier days that could allow her to continue her pursuit of Demetrius? What could he have done to give her that hope? What might have been the nature of their love? What has each risked? What has each promised?

Where is this childhood hideout that Hermia, Helena, and Lysander know about, but Demetrius does not? Where could you place it in relation to this spot in the wood? Might Demetrius and Helena have already been there and found that they missed their quarry? Or could they be still on their way there? Could Demetrius still need Helena with him to show him the way?

How could mortals find their way around this forest at night? Oberon mentions moonlight; is that good enough for the Athenians? Do they follow each other by sound? Could they feel their way along the ground? How might your lovers see? Or don't they?

Do you imagine an English forest? A Greek forest? A nightmare forest? What might the physical reality of this wood be, a forest where the normal course of the seasons has been disrupted?

Helena and Demetrius are here from the court, the city. How could each of them feel about the wood? Could either of them come prepared? Or might they have rushed out to catch the lovers as they stood? Do they feel physically out of place? How could they be dressed? How do city clothes and court appointments help or impede them as they run through a wood at night?

Demetrius is going to threaten Helena with wild beasts; will your forest be a dangerous one? How, specifically? What might each character think about the risks he or she is running in this place?

What does the future suggest about their states of mind during this scene? What might Oberon be thinking as he watches? What might Helena and Demetrius visibly do that could drive Oberon to interfere on Helena's behalf? What could happen in this scene that would make it likely that Demetrius' eventual change of heart will convince Helena?

Now that you've started to develop a detailed picture of the circumstances surrounding this scene, ask what each character might plausibly want to change? What could each be trying to get the other to do, here and now? What are the gambles each takes by actively pursuing that desire? How might the situation develop as a result of those pursuits?

Enter DEMETRIUS, HELENA *following him.*

The circumstances might suggest that it's Helena who knows her way around this place. If so, how might you explain the fact that it's the guide who is "following"? What do you imagine might have happened before this scene begins that led to this particular way of entering? What might Demetrius be trying to get Helena to do next?

What specific response could Helena be intending to evoke from Demetrius, right now, as she follows him? In detailed terms, *how* might she "pursue" him in order to win that response? Would you describe the action as a matter of escaping and pursuing? Or could it, for example, be a matter of searching and distracting him from that search? Other ideas?

What might make him stop here? Might she do something he does not expect that shows him that, if he wants to get her to change her behavior, he'll need to stop and talk to her before he leaves her? What could that be? What might Demetrius think Helena, acting in this unexpected way, has in mind? How might he want her to behave instead? How would that thought plausibly prompt him to stop and say:

DEMETRIUS

I love thee not, therefore pursue me not.

Do you imagine that Demetrius succeeds in his immediate intention? Does Helena stop what you have her doing? Could she continue? What might be the direct visible event that makes Demetrius decide to change subject at this moment?

DEMETRIUS   (Continued)

Where is Lysander and fair Hermia?

Could your Demetrius intend to get information with this line? Could Helena be acting in a way that might make him suspect she is hiding something? Or might he be saying, in effect, "Stop doing what you're doing and keep your mind on business?" Or might he wish to scare her into thinking he'll put up with her only as long as she is of use to him? Do other plausible intentions occur to you? State them in specific terms and try them out.

Demetrius goes on to declare his feelings about the missing lovers:

DEMETRIUS (Continued)
The one I'll slay, the other slayeth me.

There's no news here; Helena already knows about these feelings. So what reaction from Helena might Demetrius be intending to achieve as he chooses to state the obvious?

How could Helena choose to respond? She has no lines, but it's reasonable to propose that his next speech, when he changes the subject again and accuses her of breaking her promise, might be a reaction to something she does now. She could respond to his last line, physically at least, in a way he did not expect or want to see, some act that prompts him to say:

DEMETRIUS (Continued)
Thou tolds't me they were stol'n into this wood,
And here am I, and wood within this wood,
Because I cannot meet my Hermia.

Why might Demetrius's search have failed? Have they simply lost their way in the dark? Could Helena have led him off the path on purpose? Could Demetrius suspect so? What might each character individually believe accounts for their present predicament?

Why does he complain that he is "wood within this wood"? Some footnotes suggest that "wood" was a term that meant that he was out of his mind, others that "wood" is a pun on "wooed;" or could he be blaming Helena for the fact that he feels suddenly "wooden," frustratingly immobile? Remember, you are not looking for the meaning of the words *per se*; you are trying to improvise a speaker's *intended* meaning. So ask what Demetrius might hope Helena will do in response to his complaint.

What response could Helena give him instead? What might she do which could compel him to say again:

DEMETRIUS (Continued)
Hence, get thee gone, and follow me no more.

What could he do having said this? Will you have him set out on his own? Might you have him do something specifically designed to drive Helena away?

In fact, he accomplishes neither; both of them stay. How might that result come about? How might Helena understand what she sees him doing? What in his behavior might prompt her to choose this moment to describe her feelings to him? What might she intend to accomplish by choosing to speak in images of natural forces beyond her control?

HELENA

You draw me, you hard-hearted adamant;

What physical response could she get instead? What could Demetrius do to make her want to pursue her metaphor on to describe both his attraction and her determination:

HELENA (Continued)

But yet you draw not iron, for my heart
Is true as steel. Leave you your power to draw,
And I shall have no power to follow you.

Her description of the situation is one of a natural attraction that leaves her helpless. Is that how you imagine her? Does she necessarily act as if she had no will of her own? If not, what might she hope he'll do when he hears her claim that she can't help herself?

Demetrius responds by reducing her powerful metaphor into demeaning literal terms. Do you imagine that surprises Helena? Could she expect it? Might Demetrius hope to drive her home in tears with his next line? Or could he be trying to get her to see reason? Or intending to frighten her as he spells the situation out in his most direct language:

DEMETRIUS

Do I entice you? Do I speak you fair?
Or, rather, do I not in plainest truth
Tell you I do not, nor I cannot love you?

Whatever you choose him to hope for with this declaration of "plainest truth," he fails to get it:

HELENA

And even for that do I love you the more.

How could Demetrius react to this straightforward declaration of love? What might he intend to accomplish with that gesture? Choose something that would logically prompt Helena to try again, using even more extreme language:

HELENA   (Continued)
I am your spaniel; and, Demetrius,
The more you beat me, I will fawn on you:

Why is she talking about beating? Could he have threatened to hit her? Could he have hit her? Later in the play, Helena will tell Hermia that Demetrius spurned her with his foot and threatened far worse. Is this the moment she might have in mind? Could this speech be intended to stop some physical abuse by saying that she is determined?

Or could your Helena be speaking metaphorically again, drawing attention to her dog-like adoration of him? If so, she takes that image to disturbing lengths. What specific intention could make her refer to herself in these terms:

HELENA   (Continued)
Use me but as your spaniel, spurn me, strike me,
Neglect me, lose me; only give me leave,
Unworthy as I am, to follow you.

What might your Helen have in mind when she asks permission to follow him? Is she thinking about the immediate moment? Is she thinking of the future? What could she intend to convey to him as she speaks the word "follow"?

What could Demetrius understand her to mean? How can you imagine seeing that message received from her in his physical reaction? What response from him could lead her to go on:

HELENA   (Continued)
What worser place can I beg in your love,
And yet a place of high respect with me,—
Than to be used as you would use your dog?

The language in this passage is unsettling, which is what makes it theatrically promising. Helena abasing herself in this extreme way can become theatrically believable and striking when you imagine and reveal it as a specific act intended to move Demetrius. But you have to decide what it will move him to do. What might she hope will happen now because she said these words in the way you are imagining? Will your Demetrius accurately understand her desires? When he fights Helena's attentions, could he have the right idea about her wishes? Or might he be making a mistake when he goes on to turn her offer into a warning?:

DEMETRIUS
Tempt not too much the hatred of my spirit;
For I am sick when I do look on thee.

What literal response does he hope for with this warning? Might he accompany it with a physical insult? Or might he carry out some threat? Choose the literal ways Demetrius could pursue his immediate intention.

HELENA
And I am sick when I look not on you.

Helena turns Demetrius's insult back on him. What might she hope he'll do next? How could she back up her neat turn of phrase with physical behavior designed to get the response she wants?

How might that behavior drive him to respond by talking about the subject of sexual modesty? Will you have him be the one who first suggests this dangerous topic? Or her? How?

DEMETRIUS
You do impeach your modesty too much,
To leave the city, and commit yourself
Into the hands of one that loves you not;
To trust the opportunity of night,
And the ill council of a desert place,
With the rich worth of your virginity.

Now it's Demetrius's turn to use violent language. What could he be threatening her with? Scandal? Rape? How do you imagine he might make his threats? What way of threatening her could plausibly provoke her to answer:

HELENA
Your virtue is my privilege.

If you read ahead, you'll find that Demetrius never makes another sexual threat against Helena. Once she tells him that he is responsible for her sexual safety, he evidently concedes the point. (Is that what you imagine?) But how will her *way* of telling him convince an audience that he would choose to concede?

Could this concession be a turning point?

HELENA   (Continued)
                              . . . For that
It is not night when I do see your face,
Therefore I think I am not in the night:

Helena is no longer offering to be beaten and kicked like a dog. Her language has become soft and complimentary. What might she have seen Demetrius do that could have suggested to her that this approach might get her closer to the outcome she desires? Could Helena think she's making progress as she goes on to a fuller gentle image:

HELENA   (Continued)
Nor doth this wood lack worlds of company;
For you, in my respect, are all the world:
Then how can it be said I am alone
When all the world is here to look on me?

Could he be wavering? Could Helena be a greater threat to Demetrius as a woman for whom he discovers he still feels the vestiges of love? Or could she misunderstand? Might your Demetrius hear this speech as clear evidence that Helena will never be anything other than a doting pest to him? Can you imagine other responses, given the intentions you have in mind for Demetrius, that her words might be likely to bring about?

Consider the silent player in the scene: Oberon is watching all this. Could this be the moment when Oberon decides to help Helena get Demetrius's affections back? Could Demetrius's reaction to Helena's changed approach at this moment lead the king of the fairies to suppose his magic flower might work? How can you imagine Oberon receiving all he is learning in the course of this exchange? What intentions could appear to be occurring to him?

Imagine a chain of thought that could lead Demetrius to fall back on what is the most obvious threat of all:

DEMETRIUS
I'll run from thee and hide me in the brakes,
And leave thee to the mercy of wild beasts.

You might wonder what's stopping him; he's young, healthy, stronger, armed, and presumably faster on his feet than Helena. What might have prevented him from solving his problem in this obvious way right from the start? Does this hesitation suggest any ideas about his original purpose for stopping to talk Helena out of following him? What expectations and responses might drive him to resort to this threat *after* all his threats of physical and sexual violence have failed? How could Helena physically detain him as she says:

HELENA
The wildest beast hath not such a heart as you.

Helena has played in this wood since childhood. Will your Helena know the real risks of the forest? How could she intend to use Demetrius's attempts to scare her to her own advantage? Could she be daring Demetrius to leave her? Could she be demanding that Demetrius stop his running and face the real issue between them, rather than trying to evade responsibility by bullying her? What might she be thinking as she tells him what's to come:

HELENA   (Continued)
Run when you will, the story shall be changed:
Apollo flies, and Daphne holds the chase;
The dove pursues the griffin; the mild hind
Makes speed to catch the tiger; bootless speed,
When cowardice pursues, and valor flies.

What might Helena's message to Demetrius be in these words? Do you imagine a challenge? A threat? An appeal? A dare? What might she hope he'll do when he hears her speak?

DEMETRIUS
I will not stay thy questions . . .

What "questions?" Helena has just made statements, at least on the page. What could she have done that suggests to him that she is interrogating him? Or might he translate her speech as asking *for* something? What might that be?

What could she be trying to accomplish with her physical behavior as she speaks? What gesture prompts him to say:

DEMETRIUS   (Continued)
. . . Let me go!

Is Helena holding him? Could the tangled forest be playing a role in his attempt to escape? Might Oberon intervene at this point? If so, with what intention?

DEMETRIUS   (Continued)

Or, if thou follow me, do not believe
But I shall do thee mischief in the wood.

What kind of mischief might Demetrius have in mind? What kind of mischief might Helena fear? Are the two kinds of mischief necessarily the same? How might that understanding (or misunderstanding) bring Helena to say:

HELENA

Ay, in the temple, in the town, the field
You do me mischief.

Demetrius is promising future "mischief"; Helena turns the word back on him reminding him of past "mischief." What history is she recalling? How might he react to these reminders? Will his reaction be the one she was after? What might he do physically that impels her to try further:

HELENA   (Continued)
. . . Fie, Demetrius!

Your wrongs do set a scandal on my sex:

Which specific wrongs might she have in mind as she says these words? Wrongs in the past that led to his breaking his promise to her to pursue Hermia? Wrongs she suffered earlier in the day when her offer to betray the other couple's secret began this chase? Wrongs she has endured during the current scene? Imagine her specific accusations as she says:

> HELENA (Continued)
> We cannot fight for love, as men may do:
> We should be woo'd, and were not made to woo.

This speech stands in contrast to her last attempt to bring Demetrius around. There she defied the natural order of things ("The dove pursues the griffin," etc.). Now she seems to plead for them. What might her hopes have become by this moment?

Some editions insert a stage direction at this point to indicate that Demetrius answers this plea by leaving her. Others have her drive him off with the next line. Which do you prefer? Why? Choose the specific moment Demetrius decides to leave. Then decide which specific attempt of Helena's is the one that finally impels him to go?

> HELENA (Continued)
> I'll follow thee, and make a heaven a hell,
> To die upon the hand I love so well.

Do you imagine this is a threat? A decision? A realization? An announcement? Who might be intended to hear it? What response is it intended to provoke? Is it shouted after a fleeing Demetrius? Could it be a promise Helena makes to herself? Might Helena be sharing her discovery with the audience?

In one sense you might think that this scene hasn't changed anything, it's merely exposed a situation. The scene seems to end as it began, with Helena chasing Demetrius. But a lot of change could have occurred between them as they tried to control each other's immediate behavior. Make that change specific in your imagination. Can you imagine how the chase that ends the scene might be different from the one that began it, *because* of the conflict of intentions they've just endured? Can you see a way that that struggle might change Oberon from observer to active participant in their story? Could Demetrius's leaving and Helena's vow that she will "die upon the hand she loves so well" suggest new intentions that might have occurred to them because of their failure to achieve their original hopes? Might those new intentions intensify and inform the pursuits to come in an entirely different way?

Now consider all these questions again, both mine and those that may have occurred to you as you read; they repeat themselves. Generally, you'll find that the questions that lead you to imagine an illusion of a character thinking for him- or herself and behaving intentionally boil down to these four:

1. This act appears as if the character were trying to provoke a particular response from another character. What could that specific response be?

2. If a character is having difficulty (which is what makes plays interesting), what specific act or condition in the scene might prevent the character from achieving the response the act is intended to evoke? What is going on in this moment that gets in the way of each character's success?

3. Why might the character plausibly believe that acting in this particular way could overcome that obstacle and win the response he or she is after? What makes him or her think this behavior will work?

4. Is the character right? Does he or she win the desired response? Could that success instill a new desire? Might a failure impel your character to look for a new way of trying to get the reaction he or she wants? What future acts could be the specific result of a success or failure to achieve a particular intention?

While the questions repeat themselves, the answers will not. Here are two examples: Tyrone Guthrie, in his famous "Christmas Pantomime" production of the play at the Old Vic, asked and answered questions of this kind in a way that gave the audience an illusion of young lovers as naive and sweetly spiritual as Mendelssohn's incidental music. Helena's wish to offer Demetrius the faithful devotion of a pet was the literal extent of her desires. Demetrius appeared to be an embarrassed young man who simply wanted to get the fawning puppy dog to go away.

Peter Brook and his actors, 30 years later, imagined a very different scene. Their Helena and Demetrius were trying to fulfill their own compelling sexual desires and revulsions in a forest of tangling coils of steel wire. When that Demetrius spurned Helena, he kissed her with insulting violence and brutality. That, too, seemed entirely appropriate and consistent for this particular Demetrius; brutal kissing was shown to be a plausible way of getting the response from Helena he intended.

Imagine your own completion of the scene: Choose immediate intentions and reactions that will move the action forward in a plausible and engaging way. Imagine particular acts that reveal your characters as if they were unique human beings trying to achieve an immediate change in their situations, each persuading us that they are working toward their objectives with a mind at work.

CHAPTER 8

Discoveries and Decisions

Up until now things have been rather strained and difficult between them. Then suddenly Emilia sees Desdemona here at her most vulnerable and decides to reveal something about herself. So for the first time Desdemona sees a side of Emilia she didn't know existed, vulnerability and pain and wisdom. That is marvelous.[28]

—LISA HARROW

Demetrius and Helena pursue consistent intentions throughout their scene. What each of them wants to accomplish at the end of their scene is an extension of what each sets out to achieve at the beginning.

In other scenes, however, characters appear to change their minds. Plays are full of incidents in which characters shift from one intensely pursued intention to another, often to another that seems in direct contradiction to the first.

Lisa Harrow is describing that sort of revealing change of mind when she lays out her understanding of the "willow scene" from *Othello*. She suggests a series of steps for the process: First, her character, Desdemona, was seen pursuing an intention. In the course of that pursuit, the audience saw the character make a sudden discovery that led her to learn something (about Emelia, in this case) she never knew before. This new knowledge had the effect of changing the character's view of the circumstances of the scene; Emelia was not the person she had supposed. New circumstances require new intentions; so once her character appeared to learn something, she could appear to search for, and decide on, new things she needed to accomplish, and choose new ways to behave in order to accomplish them. By extension, these new pursuits could, in turn, lead to further discoveries, still newer intentions, and so on. Once this chain of discoveries and new intentions became clear and specific, even radical changes of mind could make sense and reveal rich, "marvelous" complexities to an audience.

Look at the radical change of mind that occurs in the following scene from *Richard III:*

(Enter GLOSTER.*)*

GLOSTER
Stay, you that bear the corse, and set it down.

ANNE
What black magician conjures up this fiend,
To stop devoted charitable deeds?

GLOSTER
Villains, set down the corse, or, by Saint Paul,
I'll make a corse of him that disobeys!

1 GENTLEMAN
My lord, stand back, and let the coffin pass.

GLOSTER
Unmannered dog! stand thou, when I command:
Advance thy halberd higher than my breast,
Or, by Saint Paul, I'll strike thee to my foot,
And spurn upon thee, beggar, for thy boldness.

(The BEARERS *set down
the coffin.)*

ANNE
What, do you tremble? are you all afraid?
Alas, I blame you not; for you are mortal,
And mortal eyes cannot endure the devil.—

Avaunt, thou dreadful minister of hell!
Thou hadst but power over his mortal body,
His soul thou canst not have; therefore, be gone.

GLOSTER

Sweet saint, for charity, be not so curst.

ANNE

Foul devil, for God's sake, hence, and trouble us not;
For thou hast made the happy earth thy hell,
Fill'd it with cursing cries and deep exclaims.
Behold this pattern of thy butcheries.—
O, gentlemen, see, see! dead Henry's wounds
Open their congeal'd mouths and bleed afresh!
Blush, blush, thou lump of foul deformity;
For 'tis thy presence that exhales this blood
From cold and empty veins, where no blood dwells;
Thy deed, inhuman and unnatural,
Provokes this deluge most unnatural,—
O God, which this blood mad'st, revenge his death!
O earth, which this blood drink'st, revenge his death!
Either, heaven, with lightening strike the murderer dead;
Or, earth, gape open wide, and eat him quick,
As thou dost swallow up this good king's blood,
Which his hell-govern'd arm hath butchered!

GLOSTER

Lady, you know no rules of charity,
Which renders good for bad, blessings for curses.

ANNE

Villain, thou know'st no law of God nor man:
No beast so fierce but knows some touch of pity.

GLOSTER

But I know none, and therefore am no beast.

ANNE

O wonderful, when devils tell the truth!

GLOSTER

More wonderful when angels are so angry.—
Vouchsafe, divine perfection of a woman,

Of these supposed evils to give me leave,
By circumstance, but to acquit myself.

ANNE

Vouchsafe, diffus'd infection of a man,
For these known evils but to give me leave,
By circumstance, to curse thy cursed self.

GLOSTER

Fairer than tongue can name thee, let me have
Some patient leisure to excuse myself.

ANNE

Fouler than heart can think thee, thou canst make
No excuse current, but to hang thyself.

GLOSTER

By such despair, I should accuse myself.

ANNE

And by despairing shalt thou stand excused;
For doing worthy vengeance on thyself,
That didst unworthy slaughter upon others.

GLOSTER

Say that I slew them not?

ANNE

Then say they were not slain.
But dead they are, and, devilish slave, by thee.

GLOSTER

I did not kill your husband.

ANNE

Why, then, he is alive.

GLOSTER

Nay, he is dead; and slain by Edward's hand.

ANNE

In thy foul throat thou liest: Queen Margaret saw
Thy murderous falchion smoking in his blood;
The which thou once didst bend against her breast,
But that thy brothers beat aside the point.

GLOSTER

I was provoked by her slanderous tongue,
That laid their guilt upon my guiltless shoulders.

ANNE

Thou wast provoked by thy bloody mind,
That never dreamt on aught but butcheries:
Didst thou not kill this king?

GLOSTER

I grant thee.

ANNE

Dost grant me, hedgehog? then, God grant me too
Thou mayst be damned for that wicked deed!
O, he was gentle, mild, and virtuous.

GLOSTER

The fitter for the King of Heaven, that hath him.

ANNE

He is in heaven, where thou shalt never come.

GLOSTER

Let him thank me, that holp to send him thither;
For he was fitter for that place than earth.

ANNE

And thou unfit for any place but hell.

GLOSTER

Yes, one place else, if you will hear me name it.

ANNE

Some dungeon.

GLOSTER

Your bed-chamber.

ANNE

Ill betide the chamber where thou liest!

GLOSTER

So will it, madam, till I lie with you.

ANNE

I hope so.

GLOSTER

     I know so.—But, gentle Lady Anne,—
To leave this keen encounter of our wits,
And fall somewhat into a slower method,—
Is not the causer of the timeless deaths
Of these Plantagenets, Henry and Edward,
As blameful as the executioner?

ANNE

Thou wast the cause, and most accurs'd effect.

GLOSTER

Your beauty was the cause of that effect;
Your beauty, that did haunt me in my sleep
To undertake the death of all the world,
So I might live one hour in your sweet bosom.

ANNE

If I thought that, I tell thee, homicide,
These nails should rend that beauty from my cheeks.

GLOSTER

These eyes could not endure thy beauty's wreck;
You should not blemish it if I stood by:
As all the world is cheered by the sun
So I by that; it is my day, my life.

ANNE

Black night o'er shade thy day, and death thy life!

GLOSTER

Curse not thyself, fair creature; thou art both.

ANNE

I would I were, to be reveng'd on thee.

GLOSTER

It is a quarrel most unnatural
To be reveng'd on him that loveth thee.

ANNE

It is a quarrel just and reasonable,
To be reveng'd on him that kill'd my husband.

GLOSTER

He that bereft thee, lady, of thy husband,
Did it to help thee to a better husband.

ANNE

His better doth not breathe upon the earth.

GLOSTER

He lives that loves thee better than he could.

ANNE

Name him.

GLOSTER

Plantagenet.

ANNE

Why, that was he.

GLOSTER

The self-same name, but one of better nature.

ANNE

Where is he?

GLOSTER

Here.

(She spits at him.)

Why dost thou spit at me?

ANNE

Would it were mortal poison for thy sake!

GLOSTER

Never came poison from so sweet a place.

ANNE

Never hung poison on a fouler toad.
Out of my sight! thou dost infect mine eyes.

GLOSTER

Thine eyes, sweet lady, have infected mine.

ANNE

Would they were basilisks, to strike thee dead!

GLOSTER

I would they were, that I might die at once;
For now they kill me with a living death.
Those eyes of thine from mine have drawn salt tears,
Shamed their aspects with store of childish drops:
These eyes, which never shed remorseful tear,
No, when my father York and Edward wept,
To hear the piteous moan that Rutland made
When the black-fac'd Clifford shook his sword at him;
Nor when thy warlike father, like a child,
Told the sad story of my father's death,
And twenty times made pause, to sob and weep,
That all the standers-by had wet their cheeks,
Like trees bedash'd with rain; in that sad time
My manly eyes did scorn an humble tear;
But what these sorrows could not thence exhale,
Thy beauty hath, and made them blind with weeping.
I never su'd to friend nor enemy;
My tongue could never learn sweet smoothing word;
But now, thy beauty is propos'd my fee,
My proud heart sues, and prompts my tongue to speak.

(She looks scornfully at him.)

Teach not thy lip such scorn; for it was made
For kissing, lady, not for such contempt.
If thy revengeful heart cannot forgive,
Lo, here I lend thee this sharp-pointed sword;
Which if thou please to hide in this true breast,
And let the soul forth that adoreth thee,
I lay it naked to the deadly stroke,
And humbly beg the death upon thy knee.
Nay, do not pause; for I did kill King Henry,—

(He lays his breast open; she
offers at it with his sword.)

But 'twas thy beauty that provoked me.
Nay, now despatch; 'twas I that stabb'd young Edward,—

(She again offers at his breast.)

But 'twas thy heavenly face that led me on.

(She lets fall the sword.)

Take up the sword again, or take up me.

ANNE

Arise, dissembler: though I wish thy death,
I will not be thy executioner.

GLOSTER

Then bid me kill myself, and I will do it.

ANNE

I have already.

GLOSTER

That was in thy rage:
Speak it again, and, even with the word,
This hand, which for thy love did kill thy love,
Shall, for thy love, kill a far truer love;
To both their deaths shalt thou be accessary.

ANNE

I would I knew thy heart.

GLOSTER

'Tis figured in my tongue.

ANNE

I fear me both are false.

GLOSTER

Then never man was true.

ANNE

Well, well, put up your sword.

GLOSTER

Say, then, my peace is made.

ANNE

That shalt thou know hereafter.

GLOSTER

But shall I live in hope?

ANNE

All men, I hope, live so.

GLOSTER

Vouchsafe to wear this ring.

ANNE

To take is not to give.

(She puts on the ring.)

GLOSTER

Look, how this ring encompasseth thy finger,
Even so thy breast encloseth my poor heart;
Wear both of them, for both of them are thine.
And if thy poor devoted servant may
But beg one favour at thy gracious hand,
Thou dost confirm his happiness for ever.

ANNE

What is it?

GLOSTER

That it may please you leave these sad designs
To him that hath more cause to be a mourner,
And presently repair to Crosby Place;
Where,—after I have solemnly interr'd
At Chertsey Monastery, this noble king,
And wet his grave with my repentent tears,—
I will with all expedient duty see you:
For divers unknown reasons, I beseech you,
Grant me this boon.

ANNE

With all my heart; and much it joys me too
To see you are become so penitent.—
Tressel and Berkley, go along with me.

GLOSTER

Bid me farewell.

ANNE

'Tis more that you deserve;
But since you teach me how to flatter you,
Imagine I have said farewell already.

(Exeunt LADY ANNE, TRESSEL, *and* BERKLEY.*)*

This scene enacts one of the most intriguing changes of mind in all of Shakespeare. In the space of 192 lines, Anne changes from cursing Richard with the foulest language in her vocabulary to accepting his ring and wishing him well. And the next time she appears in the play, she is Richard's wife and soon to be his queen. "Was ever woman in this humor won?"

Shakespeare says yes, and shows us what happens in no uncertain terms. The mystery is, *why?* How might you apply those steps implicit in Lisa Harrow's reading to this extraordinary case? What sudden discoveries might Anne make during this scene that could plausibly compel her to decide on such a radical turnabout?

Richard III is one of Shakespeare's most often produced texts. Each performance has had to find a way to resolve this mystery. Laurence Olivier, of course, defined the role for much of the twentieth century with his performances at the Old Vic and on film. Here he reports how he imagined the Lady Anne scene:

> . . . I wanted to look the most evil thing there was. But I also had to exercise some other fluid that would win Lady Anne. I decided to liberate in every pore of my skin the utmost libertinage I could imagine. When I looked at her, she couldn't look at me; she had to look away. And when she looked away, I would spend time devouring the region between her waist and upper thigh. Shocking maybe, but right, I felt. It was right for my Richard, and he was becoming my Richard by the minute.[29]

Antony Sher played a very different Richard for the RSC in 1984 and left a record of his exploration of the role in his book, *The Year of the King:*

> Richard woos Lady Anne (his most unlikely conquest in the play; I've never seen it work) by being pathetic, vulnerable. She feels sorry for him, is convinced he couldn't hurt a fly. . . .
>   Why all this obsession with him being sexy? How many severely deformed people are regarded as sex symbols?[30]

So here are two ways of solving the mystery of Anne's change of mind that were consistent with the text and judged recognizable and convincing by many spectators. Oversimplifying, of course, Olivier's Richard appeared to overwhelm Lady Anne by leading her to discover a new sexual desire. Sher's Richard appeared to turn Lady Anne around by leading her to "discover" that he was, at heart, a sensitive soul who needed her, a helpless victim of politics, propaganda, and disease, physically incapable of all the crimes she held against him. What other solutions to this mystery can you imagine?

See if a review of the physical action of the scene can suggest moments of discovery that could reveal a plausible series of steps in Anne's final capitulation. Your review of the text might look something like this:

11. 34–42 Richard successfully commands the bearers and attendants in the funeral procession to set down the body of Henry VI and to give up their march.

11. 43–47 Lady Anne, alone, steps forward and orders Richard to get out of the way and let them pass.

11. 48 Richard, with a soothing and pious appeal, stays where he is.

11. 49–61 Lady Anne publicly displays the bleeding corpse of King Henry as proof of Richard's guilt. (What might Richard's unspoken reaction be?)

11. 62–67 Lady Anne curses Richard, calling on God to destroy him for his crimes.

11. 68–74 Richard, with word-play, demonstrates an indifference to curses and accusations.

11. 75–88 Richard asks for permission to acquit himself by reasonable argument.

11. 89–92 Richard blames his brother for the death of Anne's husband.

11. 93–96 Anne rejects this claim as a lie, saying that Queen Margaret witnessed Richard's stabbing of the Prince of Wales.

11. 97–100 Richard concedes the point, blaming his loss of temper on Margaret's "slanderous tongue."

11. 101–104 Anne insists that Richard confess the murder of King Henry.

11. 105–111 Richard tells Anne that he killed these men because he desired her.

11. 111–114 Anne tries to insult Richard.

11. 115–144 Richard makes his case that Lady Anne shares his guilt for these deaths because it was her beauty that drove him to murder.

11. 144–150 Anne spits at Richard and insults his professions of love.

11. 151–172 Richard weeps, and claims that his weeping is proof of his love—all the family tragedies of the House of York cannot bring him to tears as her rejection can.

11. 173–183 Richard offers his sword and bears his breast to her as proof of his love.

11. 183 Anne drops the sword.

11. 184 Richard says she must choose—take up the sword again, or accept his proposal.

11. 185–186 Anne refuses to accept him or to kill him.

11. 187–191 Richard offers to kill himself for her sake.

11. 192–195 Anne says she wishes she knew the truth about Richard.

11. 196 Anne tells Richard to put away his sword.

11. 197–200 Richard asks Anne if her gesture means she has accepted him. She equivocates.

11. 201–205 Richard offers a ring to Anne. She takes it.

11. 206–219   Richard persuades Anne to surrender the corpse of Henry VI.

11. 220–222   Anne agrees, saying she is glad he is so penitent.

11. 223   Richard asks Anne to wish him well.

11. 223–225   Anne, with reservations, does.

Which of these incidents seems most likely to provoke Lady Anne into a discovery? Which ones might show her that her situation is radically different from the situation she presumed as she began her march to Chertsey with the body of the dead king? Mark these incidents in the text.

Now move back to an exploration of the given circumstances: Again, it's useful to begin with what is explicit and then complete a picture of the context of this scene with an improvisation of specific circumstances consistent with what is set down for you to read.

In the case of this scene, there are many sources of explicit information: the text, of course; the texts of Shakespeare's earlier plays that deal with the Wars of the Roses; and, since the subject of this play is a version of English history, those useful circumstances surrounding the situation that you can draw from the actual events, times, and places the playwright chose to use.

Presumably, the year is 1471, the year of the death of Henry VI after a lamentable and interrupted reign of 49 years. In this year, Edward, the eldest of the three surviving sons of Richard of York, began his reign as Edward IV after defeating the armies of Henry VI's queen, Margaret of Anjou, at Tewksbury. This is the year that the House of York finally defeated the principal Lancaster claimants to the throne, assumed the crown, and set about fighting among themselves.

In Shakespeare's version of the battle of Tewksbury (*3 Henry VI*), the three sons of York took turns stabbing the Prince of Wales (Henry VI's son and Lady Anne's husband) before the eyes of his mother, because she had, in her turn, personally humiliated and stabbed their father to death at the earlier battle near Wakefield. And, as noted, the previous play shows Richard of Gloster (or Gloucester) furiously killing and reviling the dead body of King Henry, the same body Anne is taking to burial now.

Who is Lady Anne? In history, she was Anne Neville, the widow of the Prince of Wales. She was a daughter of the Duke of Warwick, the man who earned the name "the kingmaker" because his shifting allegiances between the Lancaster and York claimants to the throne changed the balance of power between the warring factions. As the daughter-in-law of Henry VI, she fully expected to become queen of England when the "saintly" old king died. She was related by marriage to Richard himself; her sister was married to the Duke of Clarence, Richard's brother. She was also related to Richard by blood; her aunt, Cecily Neville, was Richard's mother, making Lady Anne and Richard first cousins. All these wars are battles to the death between members of one family.

Who is Richard? Richard of Gloucester was the third remaining son of Richard Plantagenet, Duke of York. His two elder brothers were George, the Duke of Clarence, who has switched allegiances twice during the recent battles at the behest of his father-in-law, Warwick "the kingmaker," and Edward IV, whose favoritism toward members of his wife's ambitious family, the Woodvilles, leads to much of this play's political unrest.

In the previous plays, Richard has shown himself to be a skillful warrior, overcoming his physical deformity, his crook back. Regarded as unnatural since birth, he has led a life of political skill and military malignity well suited for war. Now, in this "weak piping time of peace," he is out of place.

He has decided, therefore, to "pluck" the crown away from his brothers. To do so, he is very willing to dispose of anyone who stands between him and the throne, including his brothers and their children, each of whom has a better right of succession than he does.

The play begins in the aftermath of a change of government. Edward IV, the "sun of York," has begun his reign badly. He is an infamous womanizer. He has let Richard murder the old king unnecessarily. He has given preference to his wife's family for titles and properties won from the embittered Lancasters, leading to deadly rivalries among the Yorks. He has fallen ill recently, and he believes himself, superstitiously, to be the victim of witchcraft. "His physicians fear him mightily," Richard tells us.

The audience will have watched Richard begin his campaign for the throne by having his brother George jailed on suspicion of that witchcraft. But jailing is not enough; George must die *before* Edward, or Richard will have another family of heirs—George's children—to dispose of before he gains the throne. Richard has laid plots to this effect.

Where will you place this scene? The stage direction is "London— Another Street." The text makes it clear that Anne is taking the corpse from St. Paul's Cathedral to the monastery at Chertsey. A map will show you that St. Paul's was located at the crest of Ludgate Hill in the center of London and that Chertsey was up the river Thames some miles west of the city, a place reached by boat. Presumably, Anne is leading the funeral cortege toward some place on the embankment where they could board a boat for the trip to Henry's chosen burial ground.

When Anne surrenders the body to Richard, she agrees to go to Crosby Place, again, an actual location a few streets to the east of St. Paul's. And when Richard chooses to dispose of the body at Whitefriars rather than at Chertsey, he is referring to a priory within the city limits well away from the river and to the west of the cathedral.

There's a start on the circumstances that are explicit in the texts and from history. Now, what do those conditions suggest to you for those specific elements in the situation that the text leaves open to the imagination?

For example, we have a general location in mind, a street in medieval London situated between St. Paul's and the river. But what sort of street might you choose? Could Anne be making a public show of the burial of the deposed and murdered king in an open square alive with citizens? Or might your Richard choose to state his case in the dark privacy of a back street leading to the waterfront?

What times of year can you imagine using in this scene? Could it be set in the glorious summer Richard mentions metaphorically in his prologue? (The battle of Tewksbury was fought in April; you might find a way to put that fact to theatrical use.) Or have we, perhaps, moved on to a literal "winter of discontent"?

What ideas does time of day suggest? Could Anne choose to eulogize the dead king in the full daylight of a busy market morning? Could she have received permission to hold her obsequies on the condition that she mourn under dark of night, where no sympathetic subject might be tempted to demonstrate a challenge to the new Yorkist regime? Have the funeral rites already taken place at the Cathedral?

Or might Anne be taking the corpse to the charitable monastery of Chertsey, the only place where "holy" Henry's body and lineage will be decently acknowledged?

Make this funeral specific in your imagination. Do you picture a small procession, the pathetic remnants of a defeated court? The text mentions only two lords, Tressel and Berkley; one gentleman; bearers; and somebody with a halberd. But might it be a larger procession, defiantly proclaiming the past glories of the House of Lancaster?

Who are the men "who bear the corse"? How could Anne have secured their services? Could they be loyalists to Anne and Henry? Or might they be Chertsey monks who would charitably bury anybody? What is their stake in the confrontation they are about to witness?

How many halberds are there? One, at least, is willing to threaten Richard when he first appears. To whom could they be loyal? Are they Lancastrian veterans, perhaps? Or maybe Yorkist police? What reasons might they have to lower their weapons at Richard's command and threat?

Anne, the daughter-in-law, is the chief mourner, the sole apologist for the murdered king. How do you imagine that came about? (After all, the old queen, Henry's wife, is still at liberty in the palace.) Why is she alone, and why might she have chosen to accept this role? Do you imagine she sees this funeral as an act of holy obligation? Or could she imagine she is staging a demonstration of political defiance? What response will your Anne hope to evoke as she begins her procession through the streets of London? And from whom?

Imagine Richard. *How* could "crook-back Dickon" be deformed? Olivier wore a leg brace and a hump on his right shoulder; Antony Sher carefully studied the patterns of movement he saw in a hospital treating patients with scoliosis and kyphosis; Ian McKellen's Richard in modern dress could force himself to stand erect despite a distorted spine and an atrophied arm, but his face was scarred and there was a section of his head where his hair couldn't grow. What can you imagine?

How might this deformity affect your character's way of thinking? Richard connects his political ambitions with his being brought into this world "scarce half made up." Can you imagine a Richard who destroys his own brothers because they were born whole? Could your Richard want respect from the undeformed world? Or affection? Or revenge? (Ian McKellen says of Richard, "His mother hates him simply because he is deformed. There is no man in the world who can recover from that."[31])

How might Anne see his disability? She calls him a "lump of foul deformity," but how literally might she mean that? Do you imagine her describing him physically, morally, or both? How might her perception of his deformity affect her behavior as she discovers that he is proposing marriage?

Why might Richard want to marry Anne? He says that this marriage is part of his political calculation, but then he goes on to say he will marry her "not so much for love / As for another secret close intent / By marrying her which I must reach unto." Richard has never been coy with his audience before. What, specifically, do you imagine this "secret close intent" could be? Could it be personal? What, for example, if your Richard wanted to overcome his deformity by publicly winning this "divine perfection of a woman"? Or might his secret desire have something to do with her position at court as the Princess of Wales and as presumptive Queen from the House of Lancaster? Can you imagine moments in this scene where, as a consequence of this desire, he might be telling the simple truth? Which ones?

Now, given a list of the physical actions and reactions in the scene, a selection of those incidents where Anne might discover something important and unanticipated, and a detailed picture of the circumstances that might affect the characters' decisions, read the scene again. This time, note each step in the action and propose decisions Anne might plausibly make as she copes with the changes in circumstances that she discovers during the course of that step. Then imagine a plausible progression of thought for the character that could make her choices appear specific and likely. For example:

1. Lady Anne is startled to discover that she's been caught. The murderer himself has interrupted her mourning for the victims of her destroyed royal line. So she decides to appeal to those few Lancastrian supporters who have joined her for protection.

What thoughts could guide her choice? Some possibilities might be: "Here is Richard alone and armed only with a sword. I am protected by a number of men (how many?) and armed with halberds.

Here's a chance to kill the killer." Or: "I've been caught committing treason by publicly mourning the murdered king. Will these men fight to help me escape? I must try." Or: "Can I, like Queen Margaret, find the courage to lead men to fight against an evil enemy?"

Once you choose her train of thought, you'll be able to imagine *how* she carries out her decision to act.

2. Anne discovers that she is alone; those armed men with her are cowed by Richard. So she decides to confront Henry's murderer on her own.

How do you imagine Richard persuaded a group of men with better arms to back off? Julie Hankey, in her review of the stage history of the play, notes that in the 1979 production by the Rustaveli company, "... the seedy grotesque evil of Richard was everywhere, down to the very coffin bearers."[32] That's one solution. Here's another: Antony Sher's Richard disarmed the men using his crutches as weapons. "Richard's blows must be sadistic beyond the call of duty," Sher noted.[33]

Might your Anne think that that threat against the men wouldn't apply to her, a woman? Or to the Princess of Wales? Or to Richard's cousin? Or might she discover that, in the presence of Richard, all normal decencies become irrelevant? Might she be deciding that she has nothing to lose? Could your Anne literally believe that Richard is possessed by the devil? Or might her calls on hell be her choice of metaphor to try to stir the trembling men around her into action?

In Terry Hands' 1970 production, Lady Anne, who had been carrying a large cross in the procession, attacked Richard with it as she said, "Avaunt, thou dreadful minister of hell."[34] What character intention might have impelled that violent invention for this moment in the scene?

When she chooses to confront her enemy alone, what specific response will you have her try to evoke? And from whom? Will you have her succeed?

Richard answers Lady Anne's violence with soothing words, "Sweet saint, for charity, be not so curst." How do these words lead Anne on to uncover the body of the king? Might she see that his words have some affect on her followers? Or do you see this scene becoming an exchange between two people oblivious to those who are listening?

3. As she confronts Richard with the evidence of his butcheries, she discovers that a miracle has occurred; a dead man is bleeding as if his heart still had life. As a result, Lady Anne decides to use the miracle as public testimony that Richard is the murderer.

How do you imagine Anne will uncover the body physically? What effect might she hope uncovering the corpse will have, here and now? Could Anne choose to display the body to shock Richard out of his complacency? Could she be intending to show evidence to the "jury" of attendant gentlemen?

How do you imagine her discovering that the body has suddenly begun to bleed? In your imagination, has it? Literally? (It did in Peter Hall's production where the gory miracle occurred for all to see.) If it does, what could that miracle mean to her? Commentators on this moment in the play have noted that folkloric superstition said that murdered corpses would begin to bleed afresh in the presence of the killer. Might Anne be discovering this miraculous occurrence and publicly using her discovery as divine proof of her accusations against Richard?

Or do you imagine another Anne, one who might be speaking metaphorically at this moment? What if the body remained inert in its casket, and your Anne had the wit and the courage to attack Richard *as if* the folk tale evidence had occurred?

In either case, how do you imagine Richard responding? In the RSC production of 1979, John Wood was so fascinated by the literal appearance of fresh blood from a dead body that he went over to the corpse and tasted the blood. That's only one imaginative choice, but one that appeared so repellant to Anne and so startling to the gentlemen witnessing the scene that Anne's next choice—to call upon God for divine punishment against Richard—seemed utterly plausible.

4. Lady Anne discovers that her followers, still silent, refuse to defy Richard even in the face of the miracle. So Lady Anne decides to attack Richard herself with her fiercest curses.

Why does Anne choose to curse Richard? Do you imagine an Anne who firmly expects her curses to have tangible results? This play is full of curses, curses that come to pass in literal, if often ironic, ways; indeed Anne has, unknowingly, already cursed herself when she says, "If ever he have wife . . ." Given the superstitious world of the play, could your Anne believe that her curses are, in fact, effective weapons? What specific results could Lady Anne expect as a result of her calling on God and earth to punish Richard as horribly as he deserves?

Or do you imagine an Anne who knows that her curses are the futile gestures of a powerless woman surrounded by armed and politically ambitious men? What on-stage response would such an Anne plausibly try to achieve as she calls on heaven and earth to swallow up the murderer?

5. Lady Anne discovers that Richard is asking her to judge him. So she decides to punish him for his crimes.

This discovery changes circumstances drastically. Richard has shown no sign of vulnerability so far. All her curses and attacks seem to have had no effect. Now he is asking her to forgive him. Richard has just handed Anne a chance to strike back. What do you suppose she could have done to impel him to choose *this* moment to give her this opportunity?

What intention might drive her to answer his appeal with what Richard will call "a keen encounter of our wits"? ("Vouchsafe, divine perfection of a woman . . ." "Vouchsafe, defused infection of a man . . .", etc.) What response could she be trying to evoke from him by accusing him in words that turn his own compliments back in his face?

Then she chooses to attack more straightforwardly: "Fouler than heart can think thee, thou canst make / No excuse current, but to hang thyself." Could she think he might literally do it? Why? If so, what are the consequences of what she discovers next:

6. She discovers that Richard claims to be innocent. So she decides to trap him into a confession of guilt.

In fact, Richard might be able to convince some people that he is telling the truth in this case. The first person to stab Anne's husband on the field at Tewksbury was Richard's brother, Edward of York. But Edward's attack was quickly followed by wounds inflicted by Clarence and Richard, and Richard's was the last, fatal stroke.

But perhaps Richard suddenly learns that Anne is not as unin-
formed as he had presumed. Her version of the story is very much as
it is enacted on stage in *3 Henry VI*, Act V, Scene v:

ANNE

In thy foul throat, thou liest: Queen Margaret saw
Thy murderous falchion smoking in his blood:
The which thou once didst bend against her breast
But that thy brothers beat aside the point.

Here, with eyewitness testimony, she forces Richard to equivocate
about Margaret's irritating temper and, finally, simply grant her that
he did kill Henry VI. Is this a clear victory for your Anne? How might
she respond to this confession? How might the watching lords react?
How could that response lead to her next discovery?

7. Lady Anne discovers that Richard's confession of crime leads
to a confession of love for her. So she decides to reject his suit, spitting in his face.

How does she discover Richard's intent? Could she know instantly, as soon as he says "Your bedchamber?" Could she know it
before? Might it take her some time to absorb the enormity of what
he is proposing? Choose the exact moment, and the exact gesture or
word, when your Anne could realize that Richard is, in his way,
courting her.

Richard becomes explicit; he claims he killed her husband and her
father because he was obsessed with her beauty, and that makes her
an accessory to those murders.

Then he promises that he is a man of better nature than her husband was. That's what makes her spit at him. What will your Anne
hear in that word "nature"? Is Richard offering her greater sexual satisfaction? Or might another Anne be defending the memory of her
husband's ethical "nature"? How could Anne be influenced by the
fact that this suggestive and grotesque love scene is being witnessed
by the lords and gentlemen of the funeral procession? What might
drive your Anne, who has been so skillful and courageous in her
speech, to choose wordless spitting?

8. Lady Anne discovers that Richard will accept her spittle as
"sweet poison"; he will not be deterred. So Lady Anne decides to
drive Richard away by saying he physically disgusts her.

How could your Richard react to being spat upon? Alec Guinness drove his Lady Anne into a faint by wiping the spittle from his cheeks and licking his hand. What might your Richard calculate as he decides how to respond? How will his response drive her to cry:

ANNE
Out of my sight! Thou dost infect my eyes.

9.   Richard tells her that she has brought him to tears; could Lady Anne discover Richard weeping? Lady Anne chooses to listen to Richard's speech. Richard recounts the miseries he has suffered at the hands of the Lancastrian forces, miseries not unlike those Anne has suffered from the forces of the House of York. He claims none of this brings tears as does his love for her.

Read ahead: After Lady Anne hears this speech, she changes. She no longer fights; she hesitates, equivocates, and surrenders. What will you have her discover at this moment? Will she respond to Richard's physical presence and discover his overmastering sexuality? Will she find a new Richard, a helpless cripple who needs her help? (A number of Richards have tried to kneel before Anne during this speech, and stumbled, pathetically, because of their deformities.)

What might she be thinking when "she looks scornfully at him"? And what message might she think she receives when she hears Richard say, "Teach not thy lip such scorn; for it was made / For kissing, lady"? Might she imagine that she finds a soulmate, another victim of this pointless civil war? Or might she suddenly realize that her life is on the line, and that she has a choice between submitting herself to this tyranny masquerading as pathos or joining the long line of remorselessly eliminated Lancastrians, sacrificed to the political ambitions of the new regime? Other ideas?

10.   Lady Anne discovers that Richard is offering her the chance to kill him. Lady Anne decides that she cannot do it. She drops the sword.

Why might Richard choose this moment to give Anne a second weapon, this time a literal one, to use against him? How much of a risk could he be running? What might she do during his speech and her response to it that allowed him to think that this is the moment he might be able to force her to choose him?

Imagine the moment literally first: How could Richard take out his sword and offer it? Will Anne accept it? How? How will he bear his breast for her to strike? How will he place his distorted body at her disposal? And how might Anne respond to that sight?

How might the witnesses react? They are still there, still armed with halberds. Could their response to Richard's offer enter into Anne's thinking and choice? How?

Anne "offers at him with his sword." How might Anne go about that? And what will stop her? One of the lords? Richard? How might he do that? Or might she **be** stopped by a thought? What thought?

GLOSTER

Nay, do not pause, for I did kill King Henry,—

Some Annes, inflamed by this bald confession, have raised the sword at this point, only to weaken and stop themselves as Richard goes on to say:

GLOSTER (CONTINUED)

But 'twas thy beauty that provoked me.

The business of threatening and failing to carry through with the threat is repeated as Richard continues:

GLOSTER (CONTINUED)

Nay, now dispatch; 'twas I that stabbed your Edward,
But 'twas thy heavenly face that set it on.

But is this pattern of threats and hesitations the only one you can imagine? What else might your Anne discover as Richard offers his sword?

And then she makes a crucial choice, set out in the stage directions:

(She lets fall the sword.)

Why? What discovery might plausibly cause Anne to surrender her chance before witnesses? Does she discover that killing him would be killing a lover? Or a helpless cripple? Or might she find that Richard would physically stop her long before he was in any danger? Could she find that she was, suddenly, in mortal danger herself at that moment? How?

11. Lady Anne discovers that Richard is offering her a choice: "Take up the sword or take up me." So Lady Anne decides to try to gain some time: "That shalt thou know hereafter."

Could Lady Anne hear this offer as a threat? She says she wishes she knew his heart; might she be convinced of its sincerity? What could drive her to equivocate? Are the witnesses affecting her decision? Can you imagine a Lady Anne who *wants* to give in at this point? Or another, who is trying to find a way to escape? Could she try to leave? If so, how might Richard stop her?

12. Lady Anne discovers that Richard is offering her a ring in front of witnesses. So Lady Anne decides to accept the ring, but to deny its obvious implications of a commitment.

Where might Richard get this ring? What sort of ring do you imagine he is offering Anne? How does she understand its significance? Is it a signet ring? A ring of office? Could it signify a gift, a political allegiance, a safe conduct, or an engagement? Her understanding of its intended meaning will determine her decision to accept it as she does. Choose an understanding for the character, and imagine the specific act of accepting the ring that might plausibly follow.

In Terry Hands' production, Lady Anne accepted the ring, then picked up the corner of Richard's cape. Then, in the words of one reviewer, "In a flash she changes her mind and with no real encouragement makes a giggling date with him in the shelter of his cloak."[35] What imagined train of thought might have suggested that specific way of accepting the ring?

13. Lady Anne discovers that Richard wants the body of Henry VI. So she decides to surrender the body, saying that she's glad Richard is now penitent.

Why? Richard tells her he has "diverse unknown reasons" for wanting the corpse. Could Anne have a specific idea what those reasons are? What might she surmise? Could she believe him, that he wants the body for rites of penitence? Could she know that he needs the body for political reasons? Could she discover that it doesn't matter what his reasons are, she has absolutely no choice in the matter? Could she be offering a face-saving excuse for turning over the body of a sainted king to what she knows will be ignominious disposal?

14. She discovers, at the same time, that Richard wants her to go immediately to Crosby Palace. So Anne agrees, taking two of her attendant lords with her.

How might Anne understand the significance of going to this particular palace? Whose house is it? What does her habitation there signify? Why does she order two lords to accompany her there? What does that mean to her? What might she intend it to mean to Richard?

Why do you suppose Richard might want that body? Why is his final victory in the scene not the winning of Anne but the capture of the corpse? What reason could your Richard have for working to get the body away from Anne, Berkley, and Tressel? Can you imagine a wooing scene where the winning of Anne was Richard's *means* of getting the corpse of Henry VI away from the Lancastrians? What might that suggest?

15. Lady Anne discovers that Richard wants her to wish him well. So she decides to ask him to imagine that she has already done so.

How do you imagine this final step in Anne's change of mind? What do you suppose she has learned about Richard? Does she end the scene thinking she has found a new Richard, Richard the sincere lover, perhaps; or Richard the political ally; or Richard the helpless cripple; or Richard, the thoroughly amoral minister of hell who has terrified her into submission?

And the larger question, how could your Anne's turn-around become the defining moment of an entirely consistent character?

Aristotle says that the way we get to know a character is by watching the character choose how he or she will act. This process of finding definitive moments of discovery in a scene and improvising the story of characters deciding how they will respond to those discoveries is the way you find your own versions of Shakespeare's imaginary men and women, politicians and lovers, heroines and warriors, scoundrels, sots, clowns, sprites, ghosts, and kings.

CHAPTER 9

Spoken Action

Much of that early reading, too, was for the sounds, the rhythms, the movement of the iambic line, which to me is not instinctive but something I have to work at, a secret code to be penetrated, like music; but for this text, certainly, a wonderful route to the deeper flow of the play . . .[36]

—ZOE WANAMAKER

It's helpful to set speaking aside and consider it apart from other kinds of action on the stage. Speech, perhaps more than any other human behavior, springs directly from the workings of the mind. When we speak, even in emotionally charged situations, we have to be thinking—struggling to choose words, to find expression in both vocabulary and delivery—of how to cope with, or try to change, our situation. Our mind is racing, our choosing evident, no matter how crude or polished the result, every time we open our mouths to talk.

In the theatre, therefore, speech is the fictional act, more than any other, that leads the audience to an illusion of thoughts, intentions, discoveries, and decisions. Every time an actor speaks memorized lines, the audience must be brought to imagine that they are watching a character thinking and choosing the words they hear.

Still, it would be silly not to acknowledge that speaking Shakespeare's lines presents a special case. Not only do we have his massive vocabulary to consider (Remember those 25,000 words Peter Brook cites?), we are faced with language shaped in the conventional "heightened" forms of writing popular in his theatrical age.

Most of it uses two forms of verse, "blank (unrhymed) verse" and "heroic (rhymed) couplets." Those parts that are written in prose (about 28% of the plays' language, scholars calculate) use a prose that is astonishingly condensed, evocative, and injected into the flow of verse at precise moments when changes in action occur.

Using these forms of writing, Shakespeare has some of his characters speak with an unmatched richness of rhetorical display, artfully crafting concise appositions to make a case. Others appear to coin rhymed verses, even fully structured sonnets as they speak. Others employ the most delicate imagery; find metaphors that send echoes of recognition through an audience; or call on the rough and colorful slangs of the street, tavern, or field.

Shakespeare depended on blank verse for about 65% of his writing for the stage. In brief, this means that he wrote his speeches in "decasyllabic lines," verse lines of ten syllables, or eleven, when he chose to end his lines on an additional unstressed syllable—the so-called "feminine ending."

The "meter" of each line, its pattern of stressed syllables, is also part of the form. The lines are written in "iambic feet." That is, in five pairs of alternating unstressed and stressed syllables. ("Shall *I* com-*PARE* thee *TO* a *SUM*mer's *DAY?*")

The sentence structure of the speeches may or may not coincide with the length of a line of verse. This means that an actor, speaking these lines of verse, may or may not find a natural pause at the end of a given ten syllables; it all depends on the structure or the meaning of the sentence. If the sense of the sentence carries the speaker from line to line of verse, we have what is called a "run-on line." If the grammar or the meaning of a speech requires a break in the regular meter of the verse, a pause that falls in the middle of a line, that break is called a "caesura."

All these considerations of the artificial formation of language into verse might seem to make illusion an impossibility. How can an audience come to "believe" in a world where people speak with such concentrated poetic facility? Real people aren't like that. If we propose that an illusion is going to be based only on an audience's ability to recognize common experience in the action they see on stage, these fictional speakers of the world's most extraordinary language shouldn't be able to persuade a soul. But they do, of course, and have for centuries. Why? Here is a suggestion from Peter Brook:

> Let me make a far-fetched parallel. Picasso began to paint portraits with several eyes and noses the day he felt that to paint a profile—or to paint a full face—was a form of lie. He set out to find a technique with which to capture a larger slice of truth. Shakespeare, knowing that man is living his everyday life and at the same time is living intensely in the invisible world of his thoughts and feelings, developed a method through which we can see at one and the same time the look on a man's face and the vibrations of his brain. We know him at once as a character in real life, with a name, as though we met him on the street. But in the street his face might be blank and his tongue silent—Shakespeare's verse gives density to the portrait. This is the purpose of the striking metaphor, the purple passage, the ringing phrase. It can no longer be held for one second that such plays are "stylized," "formalized," or "romantic" as opposed to "realistic."[37]

Brook's argument begins with the recognition that plays are, after all, artificial things; they are conscious fictions, artfully constructed. The artifice of Shakespeare's language, like the abstractions of Picasso's painting, can serve to show both the recognizable surface action of a character's public shell, and, in highly concentrated form, the equally recognizable inner action of the character's private thoughts and drives, "the vibrations of his brain." Brook's claim is that carefully crafted verse for the stage, properly understood, gives an audience *more* to recognize.

Given that, how can you learn to read these texts to find, in the poet's rich use of vocabulary and carefully structured lines of verse, those "vibrations" in each character's brain?

If the form of the verse is going to help you find a character's intention in the context of a dramatic moment, then the use of the poetic stresses and vocabulary should seem to grow out of the *character's* thinking. That is, if the playwright wants to create the illusion that a carefully chosen word or phrase has particular importance to the character, he will write the line so that those are the words and phrases that are given the authority of poetic stress.

From the actor's or director's point of view, this use of structural emphasis becomes a practical resource as he or she reads. The patterns of stress in the spoken verse can point your attention precisely to otherwise invisible fictional thoughts that should appear to cause a character to speak the words set down for that character.

Look again at our example from Sonnet XVIII, "Shall I compare thee to a summer's day." The stresses of the line suggest that what is uppermost in the speaker's mind at that moment can be improvised by imagining a significance he might attach to the words "I," "compare," "to," "summer's," or "day." It would violate the meter of the verse to improvise other thoughts for him from that sentence, such as thinking centered on the word "thee," for instance.

But even the most cursory reading of a scene shows that Shakespeare's use of language is far more flexible than this rigid formula suggests. Deftly, he will shift or add stresses, juggle meters, add to or shorten a line, or create a silence.

Brook's proposal is that you read to imagine each poetic regularity and irregularity, each shift of emphasis, each jolt, each silence as illuminating the character's mind as he or she speaks. Every rich and distilled use of vocabulary, simile and metaphor, image, the onomatopoeic use of sound, alliteration, rhyme, rhetorical display, or surprise of syntax can become part of the dramatic illusion once it is understood as part of a character's apparent struggle to coin new speech to meet the needs of his or her immediate intentions, discoveries, or decisions.

That is the "code" Zoe Wanamaker is reading to crack. She wants to discover a way to speak a music in her lines as well as a literal sense; this music will create an illusion of her character's mind at work.

So, what sorts of questions should you ask to find such a revealing music? Can you discover how the choices made by Shakespeare the wordsmith carefully shape language so that it might appear to come from the imaginary consciousness of a character? How could those choices guide your improvisations about the fictional intentions at work in a scene or the course of discoveries and decisions in the action?

Consider this scene from *King Lear:*

ACT IV

Scene vi

Enter GLOUCESTER and EDGAR

GLOUCESTER

When shall I come to the top of that same hill?

EDGAR
You do climb it now: look, how we labour.

GLOUCESTER
Methinks the ground is even.

EDGAR
                    Horrible steep.
Hark, do you hear the sea?

GLOUCESTER
                    No, truly.

EDGAR
Why, then, your other senses grow imperfect
By your eyes' anguish.

GLOUCESTER
                    So may it be indeed:
Methinks thy voice is alter'd; and thou speak'st
In better phrase and matter than thou didst.

EDGAR
You are much deceiv'd: In nothing am I change'd
But in my garments.

GLOUCESTER
            Methinks you're better spoken.

EDGAR
Come on, sir; here's the place:—stand still.—How fearful
And dizzy 'tis to cast one's eyes so low!
The crows and choughs that wing the midway air
Show scarce so gross as beetles: half way down
Hangs one that gathers samphire,—dreadful trade!
Methinks he seems no bigger than his head:
The fishermen that walk upon the beach
Appear like mice; and yond tall anchoring bark
Diminish'd to her cock; her cock a buoy
Almost too small for sight: the murmuring surge,
That on the unnumber'd idle pebbles chafes,
Cannot be heard so high.—I'll look no more;

Lest my brain turn, and the deficient sight
Topple down headlong.

GLOUCESTER
Set me where you stand.

EDGAR
Give me your hand:—you are now within a foot
Of the extreme verge: for all beneath the moon
Would I not leap upright.

GLOUCESTER
Let go my hand.
Here, friend, 's another purse; in it a jewel
Well worth a poor man's taking: fairies and gods
Prosper it with thee! Go thou further off;
Bid me farewell, and let me hear thee going.

EDGAR
Now, fare you well, good sir.

(Seems to go.)

GLOUCESTER
With all my heart.

EDGAR
Why do I trifle thus with his despair
Is done to cure it.

GLOUCESTER
O you mighty gods!
This world I do renounce, and in your sights
Shake patiently my great affliction off:
If I could bear it longer, and not fall
To quarrel with your great opposeless wills,
My snuff and loathed part of nature should
Burn itself out. If Edgar live, O bless him!—
Now, fellow, fare thee well.

EDGAR
Gone, sir:—farewell,—

(GLOUCESTER leaps, and falls along.)

And yet I know not how conceit may rob
The treasury of life, when life itself
Yields to the theft: had he been where he thought,
By this had thought been past.—Alive or dead?
Ho, you sir! friend!—Hear you, sir!—speak!
Thus might he pass indeed:—yet he revives.—
What are you, sir?

GLOUCESTER

Away, and let me die.

EDGAR

Hadst thou been aught but gossamer, feathers, air,
So many fathom down precipitating,
Thou'dst shiver'd like an egg: but thou dost breathe;
Hast heavy substance; bleed'st not; speak'st; art sound.
Ten masts at each make not the altitude
Which thou hast perpendicularly fell;
Thy life's a miracle.—Speak yet again.

GLOUCESTER

But have I fall'n, or no?

EDGAR

From the dread summit of this chalky bourn.
Look up a-height;—the shrill-gorg'd lark so far
Cannot be seen or heard: do but look up.

GLOUCESTER

Alack, I have no eyes.—
Is wretchedness depriv'd that benefit,
To end itself by death? 'Twas yet some comfort
When misery could beguile the tyrant's rage
And frustrate his proud will.

EDGAR

Give me your arm:
Up:—so.—How is't? Feel your legs?
You stand.

GLOUCESTER

Too well, too well.

EDGAR

This is above all strangeness.
Upon the crown o' the cliff what thing was that
Which parted from you?

GLOUCESTER

A poor unfortunate beggar.

EDGAR

As I stood here below, methought his eyes
Were two full moons; he had a thousand noses,
Horns whelk'd and wav'd like the enridged sea:
It was some fiend; therefore, thou happy father,
Think that the clearest gods, who make them honours
Of men's impossibilities, have preserv'd thee.

GLOUCESTER

I do remember now: henceforth I'll bear
Affliction till it do cry out itself,
Enough, enough, and die. That thing you speak of,
I took it for a man; often 'twould say,
The fiend, the fiend: he led me to that place.

EDGAR

Bear free and patient thoughts.

In this scene, Edgar's intention is to save his father from despair and suicide. His hope is to lead the old man, blinded and exiled, to a place where he cannot hurt himself, then to speak to him in ways that will convince him that he is the subject of a life-saving miracle, a wonder of the "clearest gods." Speech is essentially his only resource.

Follow Edgar's story: How might both characters speak these carefully crafted lines so that Edgar's deceptions appear to convince the duke? How can the verse help you imagine an illusion of Gloucester's decisions, the workings of his mind that lead to the conversion and salvation Edgar is working to achieve?

Look at the given circumstances: Gloucester's eyes have been ripped out by his political enemies. Blind, he has been driven from his own house. Once a principal figure in Lear's court, he is now an exile, fleeing a new and despotic regime. He has betrayed a faithful son and been betrayed by the bastard son he chose to favor. Defeated, he has decided to commit suicide by throwing himself off the high cliffs of Dover. But he still has his wits about him; rather than endanger more members of his household living under the corrupt brutality of Lear's elder daughters, Gloucester has chosen to ask an escaped madman, Tom O'Bedlam, to guide him to the cliff's edge.

The madman, of course, is really Gloucester's legitimate son, Edgar, in disguise. Although disinherited and condemned by his father, he is still determined to protect the old man from both his enemies and himself. So, deceiving his father, he has brought Gloucester to this place where the ground is flat and the cliffs pose no danger.

Enter GLOUCESTER *and* EDGAR

GLOUCESTER
When shall I come to the top of that same hill?

EDGAR
You do climb up it now: look, how we labour.

GLOUCESTER
Methinks the ground is even.

EDGAR
Horrible steep.

Using his voice and his choice of language as his disguise, Edgar has to convince his blind father that flat ground is in fact a slope leading up to a cliff's edge. Gloucester may be in despair, but his remaining senses lead him to question what he is being told.

Could the use of straightforward and regular words of one syllable in Gloucester's lines suggest the thinking of a man who believes that only simple speech will penetrate the imagination of a madman? He believes himself led by an idiot, someone with good eyes but with defective reason. How might Gloucester's words sound if he were trying to get accurate information out of an undependable mind?

Edgar answers in kind; he, too, confines himself to simple, direct sentences of clear information, using regular monosyllables. But this stands in marked contrast to the cascade of contradictory images he chooses when he first appears to Lear, Kent, the Fool, and Gloucester on the heath (Act III, Scene iv). How might he think that simple speech would serve as part of his disguise in this circumstance? Or might your Edgar be making a mistake as he chooses to say these words? Gloucester is about to question Edgar's speech; could Edgar be forgetting his "role" for a moment?

At any rate, Edgar chooses to change subject abruptly:

EDGAR   (Continued)
Hark, do you hear the sea?

This line opens with a double stress: "HARK, DO you HEAR the SEA?" The sudden stress of "Hark" could have the effect of startling Gloucester, making him break off his earlier train of thought and jerk his attention to another subject. Why might your Edgar need to deliver a verbal jolt at this moment?

GLOUCESTER
No, truly.

Will you have Gloucester try to hear the sea before he answers? Or might he be trying to get back to the earlier subject, testing his own sense of balance against Tom O'Bedlam's reports of the landscape?

Again, we have a double stress in the response, "NO, TRUly." But here, the meter might suggest a different pattern of thought; Gloucester's circumstances are not Edgar's. Might these words, spoken in slow and deliberate rhythm, suggest the intent of putting the burden of proof back on Edgar? Gloucester is not making it easy for his son; again, his skepticism is intact even if his eyes are not. He always needs to test his surroundings, and why not? A blind political exile trying to escape his captors would naturally be on his guard.

EDGAR
Why, then, your other senses grow imperfect
By your eyes' anguish.

A logical argument from a madman. Here is Edgar's dilemma. If he speaks logically, Gloucester will not believe that he is mad, and the illusion Edgar seeks to create—that of Tom O'Bedlam, a man Gloucester can trust *because* he is mad—will be shattered. But if he is illogical, then Gloucester will trust his own faculties of touch and hearing. The old man will discover that the ground is flat and nowhere near the sea, that he has been deceived, and Edgar will lose his chance to save his father.

What might Edgar's thought be? The second line of the speech has four stressed syllables: "BY YOUR EYES' ANGuish." Might those insistent stresses suggest improvisations for the impulse behind the line? Might Edgar be trying to distract his father's attention away from the absent sounds of the sea by reminding him of his recent agonies? Could he be using an excessive interest in Gloucester's wounds to re-establish the illusion of the madman? What immediate solution to Edgar's dilemma does the metric stressing of the subject of Gloucester's maimed face suggest to you?

GLOUCESTER
So may it be indeed:

Gloucester seems to be acquiescing. He's accepting Edgar's diagnosis of the situation in flat and even cadence. But is he? What might happen on stage, or in his mind, that could make him say:

GLOUCESTER   (Continued)
Methinks thy voice is alter'd; and thou speak'st
In better phrase and matter than thou didst.

This new test for Edgar comes in the middle of a speech, not in response to a line written for Edgar to speak. Can you imagine an overt event, or a train of thought that could lead the old man, on his own, to jump from agreement with Edgar to testing his veracity again?

EDGAR
You are much deceiv'd: in nothing am I changed
But in my garments.

How do you imagine Edgar saying these words? What might he be trying to make happen as a result of this speech? Has he been caught off guard? Will you have him trying to recapture Tom O'Bedlam's voice? How might he be trying to protect his disguise against the questions of a man who knows him so well (his father) yet must not discover who he really is?

It is specifically his choice of language that Gloucester questions next. Find a mistake in Edgar's speech that might provoke Gloucester to say:

GLOUCESTER
Methinks you're better spoken.

Gloucester's regular meter could suggest a man who is not deceived. He seems to trust his own judgment, his own remaining senses. He wants answers.

This makes him a very unlikely candidate for the kind of deception Edgar plans. Edgar is going to have to put in an extraordinary effort if he is going to be able to convince this aware and critically intact mind that this flat ground is really the edge of Dover cliff—and convince him to the point where he will throw himself to the ground as if he were jumping to his death. Why, then, might Edgar choose to make this the particular moment of arrival at the "cliff's" edge?

EDGAR
Come on, sir: here's the place:—

How might Gloucester react to this news? Might it be his reaction which gives Edgar the impetus to say:

EDGAR   (Continued)
Stand still.

Might this interruption of the verse be a sudden outburst? What might Edgar do physically to underline his verbal illusion of immediate physical danger?

EDGAR   (Continued)
—How fearful
And dizzy 'tis to cast one's eyes so low!

Edgar's hope is that he can convince his father that Tom O'Bedlam is afraid for his own life as they stand on the cliff's edge. He needs to perform the madman's reaction to the cliff so that Gloucester will become convinced of the cliff's reality.

How might he "act" this difficult role?

EDGAR
The crows and choughs that wing the midway air
Show scarce so gross as beetles: half way down
Hangs one that gathers samphire—dreadful trade!

Gloucester has been skeptical because of the concrete details of the environment he can perceive through his unimpaired senses of touch and hearing. In addition to demonstrating Tom's fear at the height, Edgar must convince his father by combining this performance with a word picture of specific details that Gloucester cannot test, the sensation of watching birds from above or sympathetic tension at the danger facing rock-climbing gatherers. The audience must see Edgar *invent* these images as they watch, and invent them in a way that could plausibly bring suspicious Gloucester to believe.

(It might be useful to offer a note on punctuation in Shakespeare's texts, suggested by the appearance of an exclamation point at the end of "dreadful trade." Here is Peter Hall on the subject:

> . . . I've finished the *Hamlet* text, comparing Quartos and Folio; and I've managed to fillet it, with John Russell Brown's assistance, of practically all its punctuation except what is essential to sense.
>
> Shakespeare's text is always absurdly over punctuated; generations of scholars have tried to turn him into a good grammarian. Even the original printed texts are not much help—the first printers popped in some extra punctuation. When punctuation is just related to the flow of the spoken word, the actor is liberated.[38]

Any two editions of this scene will bear Hall's observations out; the varieties of punctuation are endless. For our purposes, it's better to look for a dramatic sense of the speech—the illusion of a character intending to evoke a specific response through these words—and to the direction the metric structure of the verse offers as it is spoken for guidance.)

EDGAR (Continued)

Methinks he seems no bigger than his head:
The fishermen that walk upon the beach
Appear like mice; and yond tall anchoring bark
Diminish'd to her cock; her cock a buoy
Almost too small for sight:

So far, Edgar's word-picture has been coined to appeal to Gloucester's visual imagination. He's about to take another risk, choosing words that will appeal to a sense that Gloucester *does* have, his sense of hearing.

EDGAR   (Continued)

the murmuring surge,

That on the unnumber'd idle pebbles chafes,

Cannot be heard so high.—

Here, again, Edgar must appear to *choose* the onomatopoeia of his speech. The sounds of his speaking such words as "murmuring," "surge," and "chafes" echo the sounds of waves washing over a pebble beach, substituting for the sounds Gloucester is "too far away" to hear.

What effect might these spoken sounds have on Gloucester? How might the old man respond physically, provoking Edgar to break off his intense description of the imaginary cliff?

EDGAR   (Continued)

I'll look no more;

Lest my brain turn, and the deficient sight

Topple down headlong.

The word-picture succeeds; Gloucester gives up his skeptical questioning and accepts Edgar's description as truth:

GLOUCESTER

Set me where you stand.

EDGAR

Give me your hand:—

Once the illusion is accepted as truth by blind Gloucester, both characters' needs change. What does the fact that they immediately change their speech to efficient single syllables suggest to you about their thoughts at this moment?

EDGAR   (Continued)

you are now within a foot

Of the extreme verge: for all beneath the moon

Would I not leap upright.

The iambic stress falls on the word "I," and not on the word "not"; "I" is the important word to Edgar. How might that emphasis suit Edgar's immediate purposes?

GLOUCESTER
Let go thy hand.
Here, friend, 's another purse; in it a jewel
Well worth a poor man's taking: fairies and gods
Prosper it with thee! Go thou further off;
Bid me farewell, and let me hear thee going.

Five short statements jumping from subject to subject; Gloucester commands Tom, rewards him, blesses him, tells him to move
away, and tests his veracity, all in four and one half lines. Presumably Gloucester, now that he believes he's at the cliff's edge, does not
want to be rescued by a well-meaning idiot. What might this bunch-
ing of short, disconnected sentences suggest about his thinking in this
moment of decision?

EDGAR
Now, fare you well, good sir.

(Seems to go.)

Edgar has to create another illusion—that Tom O'Bedlam is leaving. How will you have him do that? What sounds will he make to
convince Gloucester he is now alone on the cliff's edge?

GLOUCESTER
With all my heart.

How might Gloucester accept Edgar's invention? Might he say
these lines to himself, wishing himself fair passage as he dies? Might
he be accepting Edgar's good wishes as a way of encouraging "Tom"
to go further away?

EDGAR
Why I do trifle thus with his despair
Is done to cure it.

To whom will you have Edgar speak? Many editions of the play
insert a stage direction, "ASIDE," for this line. The aside is a prob-
lematic convention in theatrical reading. Stanislavski wrote of what
he called "self communion"; in an aside, an actor, to avoid speaking
directly to the audience and breaking the illusion of the "fourth wall,"

should perform these lines as if the character were conversing with an alter ego inside himself. The aside, like the soliloquy, should be understood as an inner struggle, an active attempt to resolve an inner dilemma, to reach a decision.[39]

John Barton, however, counsels actors to think of this convention as if the character were sharing his thoughts with an ever-present audience.[40] The theatre's artificiality should be openly declared and put to artistic use. In this, Barton is arguing for a theatrical understanding analogous to Peter Brook's idea when he asks that a character in a Shakespearean play be seen as an abstract art object like a Picasso painting, a theatrical representation that dramatizes the inner action of thinking as well as the external action of physical behavior.

Each company of actors has to choose between these two perspectives because the target of this kind of speech, be it alter ego or present audience, will determine, to a great extent, the way the speech must be spoken.

GLOUCESTER
O you mighty gods!
This world I do renounce, and in your sights
Shake patiently my great affliction off:
If I could bear it longer, and not fall
To quarrel with your great opposeless wills,
My snuff and loathed part of nature should
Burn itself out.

Here, the "target" seems unambiguous; Gloucester is calling out to the "mighty gods." But who are they? Do you imagine this scene in a pre-Christian world governed by the whims of pagan deities? Is suicide a sin in Gloucester's mind? Might Gloucester feel the need to justify his act to his gods? Might he be defying the tenets of his own faith? Could he be trying to bargain with the gods that rule his earth?

See if you can discover some clues in the shape of the language he uses: Why might Gloucester choose to speak in one grand sentence made of two sustained pieces of oratorical argument (in marked contrast to the economically direct single syllables of his earlier exchanges)? What could this change of voice suggest about his immediate thoughts and intentions?

GLOUCESTER   (Continued)
If Edgar live, O bless him!—

Might Gloucester think that these are to be his last words? He knows, now, the injustice he did when he chose to believe his other son, Edmund, over his legitimate issue. Might we hear him cry these words as his reason for destroying himself? Or might you imagine that, they, too are intended as Gloucester's petition to higher powers? If so, what might interrupt him?

GLOUCESTER   (Continued)
Now, fellow, fare thee well.

EDGAR
Gone, sir:—farewell—

What story will you choose for this moment of hesitation? When Edgar hears his name blessed by his father, might he do something that betrays his location to Gloucester? What? Might Gloucester be wishing "Tom" farewell to test out his location? Has Edgar backed off enough to satisfy the duke? Might Edgar then stage a second deception with his voice and the sounds of his walking to assure Gloucester his end will be a private one? How might Edgar set his father's mind at ease, so that the next element in the text, the stage direction, seems plausible?

(GLOUCESTER *leaps, and
falls along.*)

How do you imagine this fall? Could Gloucester "leap up" as Edgar warned him not to do? Could the emotional tension of the moment cause him to faint? All we know for sure is that the fall, and Gloucester's stillness on the ground must plausibly provoke Edgar to say:

EDGAR   (Continued)
And yet I know not how conceit may rob
The treasury of life, when life itself
Yields to the theft.

It seems unlikely that Tom O'Bedlam would use such a reasoned metaphor. So might you have Edgar using his own voice at this moment? What might he see that would allow him to drop his disguise? Or provoke him to? How might he make that discovery as he approaches the unconscious body of his father?

To whom will you have him speak? Again, the issue of the object of speaking an aside comes up. Why might Edgar feel the need to reveal his inner doubts at this moment? To whom will you have him make this revelation?

EDGAR   (Continued)
　　　　. . . had he been where he thought,
By this had thought been past.—Alive or dead?

What impulse might drive Edgar to choose to speak in the ironic balance of antithetical uses of the word "thought?" Then, what discovery might compel him to drop all embellishment of speech and simply ask, "Alive or dead?"

EDGAR   (Continued)
Ho, you sir! friend!—Hear you, sir!—speak!
Thus he might pass indeed:

What voices will you choose for Edgar as he speaks these words? Will he assume his old disguise of Tom O'Bedlam? Is he moving on to the next disguise, the stranger on the beach? Might he panic at some point, trying to revive Gloucester in his own voice?

EDGAR   (Continued)
　　　　—yet he revives.—

How does Gloucester revive? Has Edgar done something to wake him up? Has his fainting spell simply run its course? Does some sudden noise break into his consciousness? Imagine the story of Gloucester's false death in specific terms.

EDGAR   (Continued)
What are you, sir?

What is Edgar's new voice? How might he establish this second character he has decided to play with his speech?

GLOUCESTER

Away, and let me die.

Imagine Gloucester's thoughts as he says this line. Where might he think he is? To whom does he think he is speaking? Do you imagine this line a command? An appeal?

EDGAR

Hadst thou been aught but gossamer, feathers, air,
So many fathom down precipitating,
Thou'dst shiver'd like an egg:

What does the language of this answer suggest about Edgar's new disguise? Might the succession of ever lighter metaphors ("Gossamer, feathers, air") suggest he's portraying the attempts of a simple man searching for words to report a miracle he has just witnessed? Does his use of nautical distances ("So many fathom down") suggest a man of the sea? If so, how might Edgar use his voice and his language to convince Gloucester that Tom O'Bedlam has wandered off at the top of a cliff and that Gloucester is now at the base of the cliff in the company of one of the "fishermen that walk upon the beach?"

EDGAR (Continued)

but thou dost breathe;
Hast heavy substance; bleed'st not; speak'st; art sound.

With short phrases and antithetical imagery, might Edgar pretend to be discovering this miraculous solidity in the body of a man who has fallen harmlessly? How, specifically, could Edgar choose to create this illusion for his father's ears and sense of touch?

EDGAR (Continued)

Ten masts at each make not the altitude
Which thou hast perpendicularly fell:

Again, Edgar chooses to speak using the language of sailors. Why might he feel the need to reinforce the illusion of his new role at this moment?

EDGAR

Thy life's a miracle.—Speak yet again.

This is, of course, the core of Edgar's plan, to save his father's life from suicide by convincing the duke of the value of that life. The staging of this "miracle" is Edgar's way of making his father re-think his despair. What way of speaking these seven words, which naturally place stress on "life" and "miracle," might have the best chance of accomplishing that change of heart?

GLOUCESTER

But have I fall'n, or no?

Notice again; whenever Gloucester wants information, he chooses to speak in terse syllables, stressing those words that call for facts and abruptly interrupting Edgar's word-pictures.

EDGAR

From the dread summit of this chalky bourn.
Look up a-height: The shrill-gorg'd lark so far
Cannot be seen or heard: do but look up.

Here you have a stage picture to imagine: How could Edgar, even playing the role of a stranger, appear likely to have missed the fact that Gloucester is blind? Gloucester's blinding is among the most violent and repellent scenes in all drama (Act III, Scene vii). How might Edgar have arranged things so that Gloucester's mutilated face would never be seen by the "stranger" he is playing? Throughout this scene, Gloucester has been asking for tangible evidence to convince himself of the truth of the various disguises Edgar has assumed. How would Edgar choose to arrange this scene, physically, so that skeptical Gloucester would accept Edgar's invitation to look as proof that he had met a new person who knew nothing of his injuries?

Edgar's staging must work:

GLOUCESTER

Alack, I have no eyes.—

Here's an incomplete line; it's missing two feet. Why? Might that silence be filled by Gloucester's act of revealing his shockingly de-

stroyed eyes to this new "stranger"? Imagine that moment in detail.
And imagine Edgar's performance of the "stranger's" response.

Where will you place the precise moment when Gloucester accepts the fact that he is not dead, but rather in the same state of
wretchedness he was in before he summoned his courage and energy
to kill himself? Might that important realization occupy the moment
of silence as well?

> GLOUCESTER　(Continued)
> Is wretchedness deprived that benefit
> To end itself by death? 'Twas yet some comfort,
> When misery could beguile the tyrant's rage
> And frustrate his proud will.

To whom do you imagine Gloucester is speaking? The stranger?
The "mighty gods"? Might it be his turn to share thoughts with an
audience or an alter ego? What response might he hope for as he
speaks these lamenting words? And from whom?

> EDGAR
> Give me your arm.
> Up:—so.—How is't? Feel you your legs? You stand.

The playwright leaves time, marked by the short syllables of these
instructions, for the physical business of getting the old man up on his
feet. Imagine that moment. Specifically, how might Edgar get his father
to stand? What specific difficulties might each man have to overcome?

> GLOUCESTER
> Too well, too well.

A repetition. What response might Gloucester hope for as he re-
peats these long syllables of failure?

> EDGAR
> This is above all strangeness.

Irregular syllables break into the regular pulse of Gloucester's
line. How might Edgar be planning to break into the pattern of
Gloucester's despair?

> EDGAR　(Continued)
> Upon the crown o' the cliff what thing was that
> Which parted from you?

GLOUCESTER
A poor unfortunate beggar.

At what instant might Edgar conceive of his idea of a fantasy demon? And how might you use the language to allow an audience to see it appeal to Gloucester's reawakening mind?

EDGAR
As I stood here below, methought his eyes
Were two full moons; he had a thousand noses,
Horns whelk'd and wav'd like the enridged sea:
It was some fiend:

Here, Edgar paints a nightmare image, a gargoyle picture from the sea that stands in marked contrast to the assembly of literal details and measurements he used earlier to complete the illusion of the cliff in Gloucester's imagination. How might he introduce this fantastical story so that it could believably convince the skeptical lord that a supernatural intervention has occurred?

And why do you suppose he might choose to stress the words "happy father" at this moment?

EDGAR   (Continued)
therefore, thou happy father,
Think that the clearest gods, who make them honours
Of men's impossibilities, have preserv'd thee.

GLOUCESTER
I do remember now: henceforth I'll bear
Affliction till it do cry out itself,
Enough, enough, and die.

Gloucester makes his decision to live because he suddenly remembers something. How might he absorb and respond to this new thought?

GLOUCESTER   (Continued)
That thing you speak of,
I took it for a man; often 'twould say,
The fiend, the fiend: He led me to that place.

Earlier in the play, when Kent, Lear, and Gloucester first met Edgar in his disguise as Tom O'Bedlam, Edgar had raved against a tormenting fiend whom he called Shmulkin. Gloucester remembers this now, makes the connection in his mind and is reporting his realization to the "stranger." A stranger on the beach could not have known Tom O'Bedlam or his friends, so his naive testimony must be true. Gloucester decides to live because he thinks he has "discovered" the miraculous solution to the mystery of his own salvation for himself.

And, again, just as he has whenever he is seeking or describing simple and literal fact, Gloucester chooses to express his sudden realization in simple and direct lines, in a naturally regular rhythm and in words of few syllables. What might that particular use of language suggest about the nature of Gloucester's belief in his miracle?

EDGAR

Bear free and patient thoughts.

Edgar has succeeded. How might he mark his victory? Which voice might he use? What response does he hope for from his father as he says this restful sentence, gently stressing freedom and patience?

And then what could happen? How do you imagine this scene ending? What might be the action that the arrival of Lear, "mad and bedecked with weeds" but with his eyes intact, is going to interrupt?

There are many stories for you to imagine in the sounds and meters of speaking indicated in Shakespeare's rich verse. Learn to read these texts with your ears open. Discover the sounds the playwright's lines allow. Then imagine all the dimensions of action, circumstance, and shifting intentions those sounds can suggest for the stage.

CHAPTER 10

Time

And there's a fourth character in the scene. There's old Time as well.[41]

—TONY CHURCH

A play—any work of art that is performed—consumes time. It takes a certain amount of time to see and hear a play, "Two hours' traffic of our stage," says Shakespeare's Chorus, setting a pace few productions of *Romeo and Juliet* can match.

A play also represents time; fictional time is part of the story the play reveals to an audience. Each play uses its theatrical resources to portray a fictional time in history, its own version of seasons, and its setting of the hours of the day. Audiences accept many artificially depicted conditions of time, for example, that minutes represent years, or that characters feel time passing too slowly or too fast. As you've discovered by now, fictional time, like a "fourth character," influences what all the other characters appear to do; time is always a factor, always among the most influential of the given circumstances.

In addition, events in a play have rhythm, pace, and tempo when they are performed. Speeches, sounds, and gestures can appear on the stage as lyric passages or as jarring blows to the senses. Incidents can occur in rapid, accelerating succession, or, like an *adagio* in music, they can stretch out solemnly. They can startle an audience with their sudden appearance, or they can unfold with gentle and languorous regularity. In other words, plays not only consume time and represent time; they, like music, also *organize* time.

Consuming real time is part of the nature of the theatre. Representing fictional time on the stage is part of completing the given circumstances of the action. Now, look at the third theatrical use of time; how will your imaginative consideration of the rhythm of events get you closer to improvising a completed illusion for the text in your hand?

Consider the following scene from *Twelfth Night*. As you read, see if the incidents suggest rhythms to you. Do some parts feel as if they should pass slowly? Others fast? Do you imagine an even rhythm in some places and an erratic one in others? When do you think the tempo might change from one pace to another?

Note your sense of the rhythmic patterns of action implicit in the text. Then ask why. What have you found in the text that leads you to imagine those rhythms? And what, once you have a rhythm in mind, does that rhythm suggest to you about the nature of the action you're imagining? What story might the rhythms tell?

Scene iii

Enter Sir TOBY BELCH *and Sir* ANDREW AGUECHEEK

SIR TOBY

Approach, Sir Andrew: not to be a-bed after midnight is to be up betimes; and *diluculo surgere,* thou know'st.

SIR ANDREW

Nay; by my troth, I know not: but I know to be up late is to be up late.

SIR TOBY

A false conclusion; I hate it as an unfilled can. To be up after midnight, and to go to bed then is early: so that to go to bed after midnight is to go to bed betimes. Does not our lives consist of the four elements?

SIR ANDREW

Faith, so they say; but I think it rather consists of eating and drinking.

SIR TOBY

Thou art a scholar; let us therefore eat and drink.—Marian,
I say!—a stoop of wine.

Enter CLOWN

SIR ANDREW

Here comes the fool, i' faith.

CLOWN

How now, my hearts? Did you never see the picture of we
three?

SIR TOBY

Welcome, ass. Now let's have a catch.

SIR ANDREW

By my troth, the fool has an excellent breast. I had rather
than forty shillings I had such a leg; and so sweet a breath
to sing as the fool has. In sooth, thou wast in very
gracious fooling last night when thou spokest of Pigrogromitus of the Vapians passing the equinoctial of Queubus; 'twas
very good, i' faith. I sent thee sixpence for thy leman.
Hadst it?

CLOWN

I did impeticos thy gratillity; for Malvolio's nose is no
whipstock. My Lady has a white hand, and the myrmidons are
no bottle ale houses.

SIR ANDREW

Excellent! Why, this is the best fooling, when all is done.
Now, a song.

SIR TOBY

Come on; there is sixpence for you: Let's have a song.

SIR ANDREW

There's a testril of me too: If one knight give a—

CLOWN

Would you have a love-song, or a song of good life?

SIR TOBY

A love-song, a love-song.

SIR ANDREW

Ay, ay; I care not for good life.

CLOWN

(Singing.)

O, mistress mine, where are you roaming?
O stay and hear; your true love's coming,
   That can sing both high and low:
Trip no further, pretty sweeting;
    Journeys end in lovers' meeting
      Every wise man's son doth know.

SIR ANDREW

Excellent good, i' faith.

SIR TOBY

Good, good.

CLOWN

What is love? 'tis not hereafter;
Present mirth hath present laughter;
   What's to come is still unsure:
In delay there lies no plenty;
    Then come kiss me, sweet and twenty,
      Youth's a stuff will not endure.

SIR ANDREW

A mellifluous voice, as I am true knight.

SIR TOBY

A contagious breath.

SIR ANDREW

Very sweet and contagious, i' faith.

SIR TOBY

To hear by the nose, it is dulcet in contagion. But shall
we make the welkin dance indeed? Shall we rouse the night
owl in a catch that will draw three souls out of one weaver?
Shall we do that?

SIR ANDREW

An you love me, let's do 't: I am a dog at a catch.

CLOWN

By'r lady, sir, and some dogs will catch well.

SIR ANDREW

Most certain: Let our catch be, *Thou knave.*

CLOWN

Hold thy peace, thou knave, knight? I shall be constrained in't to call thee knave, knight.

SIR ANDREW

'Tis not the first time I have constrained one to call me knave. Begin, fool; it begins *Hold thy peace.*

CLOWN

I shall never begin if I hold my peace.

SIR ANDREW

Good, i' faith! Come, begin.

(They sing a catch.)

Enter MARIA.

MARIA

What a caterwauling do you keep here! If my lady have not called up her steward, Malvolio, and bid him turn you out of doors, never trust me.

SIR TOBY

My Lady's a Cataian, we are politicians; Malvolio's a Peg-a-Ramsay, and *Three merry men be we.* Am I not consanguineous? am I not of her blood? Tilly-valley, lady! *There dwelt a man in Babylon, lady, lady.*

(Singing.)

CLOWN

Beshrew me, the knight's in admirable fooling.

SIR ANDREW

Ay, he does well enough if he be disposed, and so do I too; he does it with a better grace, but I do it more natural.

SIR TOBY

(Singing.)

O, the twelfth day of December,—

MARIA

For the love 'o God, peace.

Enter MALVOLIO

MALVOLIO

My masters, are you mad? or what are you? Have you no wit,
manners, nor honesty, but to gabble like tinkers at this
time of night? Do ye make an ale-house of my lady's house,
that ye squeak out your coziers' catches without any mitiga-
tion or remorse of voice? Is there no respect of place,
persons, nor time, in you?

SIR TOBY

We did keep time, sir, in our catches. Sneck up!

MALVOLIO

Sir Toby, I must be round with you. My lady bade me tell
you that though she harbours you as her kinsman she's
nothing allied to your disorders. If you can separate
yourself and your misdemeanours, you are welcome to the
house; if not, an it would please you to take leave of her,
she is very willing to bid you farewell.

SIR TOBY

Farewell, dear heart, since I must needs be gone.

MARIA

Nay, good Sir Toby.

CLOWN

His eyes do show his days are almost done.

MALVOLIO

Is't even so?

SIR TOBY

But I will never die.

SIR ANDREW

Sir Toby, there you lie.

MALVOLIO

This is much credit to you.

SIR TOBY

Shall I bid him go?

CLOWN

What an if you do?

SIR TOBY

Shall I bid him go and spare not?

CLOWN

O no, no, no, no, you dare not.

SIR TOBY

Out o' tune? Sir, ye lie.—Art any more than a steward?
Dost thou think, because thou art virtuous, there shall be
no more cakes and ale?

CLOWN

Yes, by Saint Anne; and ginger shall be hot i' the mouth,
too.

SIR TOBY

Thou'rt i' the right.—Go, sir, rub your chain with crumbs:—
A stoop of wine, Maria!

MALVOLIO

Mistress Mary, if you prized my lady's favour at anything
more than contempt, you would not give means for this
uncivil rule: she shall know of it, by this hand.

(Exit.)

MARIA

Go, shake your ears.

SIR ANDREW

'Twere as good a deed as to drink when a man's a-hungry, to
challenge him to the field, and then to break promise with
him and make a fool of him.

SIR TOBY

Do't, knight: I'll write thee a challenge; or I'll deliver
thy indignation to by word of mouth.

MARIA

Sweet Sir Toby, be patient for to-night; since the youth of
the count's was to-day with my lady, she is much out of
quiet. For Monsieur Malvolio, let me alone with him; if I
do not gull him into a nayword, and make him a common
recreation, do not think I have wit enough to lie straight
in my bed. I know I can do it.

SIR TOBY

Possess us, possess us; tell us something of him.

MARIA

Marry, sir, sometimes he is a kind of Puritan.

SIR ANDREW

O, if I thought that, I'd beat him like a dog.

SIR TOBY

What, for being a Puritan? Thy exquisite reason, dear
knight?

SIR ANDREW

I have no exquisite reason for't, but I have reason good enough.

MARIA

The devil a Puritan that he is, or anything constantly but a
time pleaser: an affection'd ass that cons state without
book and utters it by great swarths; the best persuaded of
himself, so crammed, as he thinks, with excellences, that it is his
ground of faith that all that look on him love him; and on that
vice in him will my revenge find notable cause to work.

SIR TOBY

What wilt thou do?

MARIA

I will drop in his way some obscure epistles of love;
wherein, by the colour of his beard, the shape of his leg,
the manner of his gait, the expressure of his eye, fore-
head, and complexion, he shall find himself most feelingly
personated. I can write very like my lady, your niece; on a
forgotten matter we can hardly make distinction of our
hands.

SIR TOBY

Excellent! I smell a device.

SIR ANDREW

I have't in my nose too.

SIR TOBY

He shall think, by the letters that thou wilt drop, that
they come from my niece, and that she is in love with him.

MARIA

My purpose is, indeed, a horse of that colour.

SIR ANDREW

And your horse now would make him an ass.

MARIA

Ass, I doubt not.

SIR ANDREW

O 'twill be admirable.

MARIA

Sport royal, I warrent you. I know my physic will work with
him. I will plant you two, and let the fool make the third,
where he shall find the letter; observe his construction of
it. For this night, to bed, and dream on the event. Farewell.

(Exit.)

SIR TOBY

Good night, Penthesilea.

SIR ANDREW

Before me, she's a good wench.

SIR TOBY

She's a beagle true bred, and one that adores me. What o' that?

SIR ANDREW

I was adored once too.

SIR TOBY

Let's to bed, knight.—Thou hadst need send for more money.

SIR ANDREW
If I cannot recover your niece I am a foul way out.

SIR TOBY
Send for money, knight; if thou hast her not in the end call me Cut.

SIR ANDREW
If I do not, never trust me; take it how you will.

SIR TOBY
Come, come; I'll go burn some sack; 'tis too late to go to
bed now: come knight; come knight.

(Exeunt.)

In broad terms, the physical action of the scene has six steps: 1)
Toby and Andrew enter and talk about drinking and finding their
way to bed; 2) Feste enters, entertains them, and helps whip the sots
up into a noisy dance and song; 3) Maria enters to hush them up before Malvolio arrives; 4) Malvolio enters, tries and fails to assert his
authority; 5) Malvolio leaves, and Maria enlists the others into a plot
to humiliate Malvolio; and 6) Maria exits, leaving the sleepy knights
to carry on as best they can.

Thinking of these incidents in terms of their rhythm, you might
decide to have the "time signature" for the first step be determined
by Sir Andrew's search for a comfortable place to curl up and go to
sleep, for example. Then you might choose changing tempi for the
second step from the progression of Feste's songs—warming up the
sots to attack Malvolio by giving them first a love song and then a
rowdy catch to follow—and so on.

What you are doing, of course, is finding a rhythm for a section
of the action by improvising given circumstances and characters' intentions for each incident: If Andrew is sleepy (a given circumstance), the events in that step in the action could be imagined happening in the sleepy rhythm of a man about to nod off. If Feste
wants to wake people up (an intention), you could reasonably suppose he'd make things happen on stage in an accelerating rhythm
that could have that desired effect. Discovering specific given circumstances and intentions usually suggests rhythms for the action
your audience will see.

But don't settle for a single rhythm for any section of the scene. These six steps are full of contrasting incidents; characters make discoveries, circumstances alter and intentions change. So each section can be alive with rhythmic variation as the action develops.

What you will find is that as you choose specific intentions and circumstances for a moment of action, specific rhythms of behavior will come to mind; by the same token, as you sense a variation in rhythm on stage, new ideas about the characters' intentions, circumstances, discoveries, and decisions will come into focus. The manipulation of rhythm is one of the theatre's most effective ways of articulating each character's reasons for behaving as you imagine they do.

Try it:

Enter Sir TOBY BELCH *and Sir* ANDREW AGUECHEEK

SIR TOBY

Approach, Sir Andrew;

What characters' intentions could inform this section of the scene? Might this scene be about Sir Toby trying to keep Sir Andrew awake so he will have a companion to drink with? Might it rather be the first step in a plan by Sir Toby to pick a fight with Malvolio? Or could it be about Toby trying to wheedle some more money out of Andrew? Or is this a scene where Toby dares Sir Andrew to set foot inside the adored Olivia's house for the first time? Choose.

Now ask some practical questions about the context: Where, in Olivia's house, might this scene take place? Where might you put these two knights in relation to the sleepers in this house? Will you set this scene in the garden of the house? The kitchen courtyard? A street under Olivia's window? Up on the roof? Design a geography for this scene that could plausibly contain the action and offer the most engaging setting for the specific story you have chosen to explore.

Now see if ideas about the rhythm of the action come to mind as you read: How might these two men be moving in this setting? What might appear to determine their rhythm of walking, the time of night? The amount of drink they have consumed? The prank they intend to pull? Could they be they moving in the tempo of men who are tiptoeing into a place where they should not be?

SIR TOBY   (Continued)
               . . . not to be a-bed after midnight
is to be up betimes; and *diluculo surgere,* thou know'st.

"Diluculo surgere" is part of a Latin popular saying that is something like "Early to bed, early to rise. . . ." What might the rhythm of Toby's quoting this old saw tell you about his intentions? Might Toby be trying to wake Andrew up? Or amuse him? Or persuade him to do something in response?

With what pace might your Andrew respond? Might he spend time trying to sort out his muddled thoughts? Could his attention be on the chance he might be caught in his lady's garden at night? Is he cutting Toby's rhythm off so that he can get back to his own safe bed as he says:

SIR ANDREW
Nay; by my troth, I know not: But I know to be up late is
to be up late.

SIR TOBY
A false conclusion; I hate it as an unfilled can. To be up
after midnight, and to go to bed then is early: so that to go
to bed after midnight is to go to bed betimes.

A couple of rhythms might suggest themselves: Sir Andrew might be slowly trailing off in his speech, slipping away as he falls asleep. Sir Toby might then jump in, trying to wake him and engage him in the fun of a silly argument. Or perhaps Sir Andrew might be speaking with the deliberate regularity of a man trying to regain control of his drunken speech, and Sir Toby might respond with a tongue-twisting conundrum for the fun of watching his victim lose his way again. Other ideas?

SIR TOBY   (Continued)
. . . Does not our lives consist of the four elements?

When a character discovers a reason to speak on a new subject, the odds are he will also have a reason to speak in a different rhythm. Again, imagine your way back from this shift of subject to the event that brings it about. What might Sir Andrew do that could impel

Toby to start a new argument, shifting from the subject of the abstractions of the clock to the elements of air, fire, water, and earth? And how might Sir Andrew's action determine the rhythm, as well as the words, Sir Toby might choose for his speech?

SIR ANDREW

Faith, so they say; but I think it rather consists of eating
and drinking.

Might Sir Andrew be speaking in the insistent tempo of a man accusing Sir Toby of taking advantage of him? Could he be speaking in the rhythm of a man who has just discovered a funny remark of his own to say? Is he slurring his way through a moment of self-pity? Could he suddenly discover a new irony to his situation? Or could he again be sliding off into unconsciousness?

As a result, might Sir Toby be speaking with the urgency of a clever panhandler who doesn't want to let his meal ticket get away? Or might this be Sir Toby's second attempt to jolt Sir Andrew and wake him up?

SIR TOBY

Thou art a scholar; let us therefore eat and drink.—Marian,
I say!—a stoop of wine.

Here you have a few more practical choices to make. What might lead your Sir Toby to expect that Maria is available to serve wine at this time of night? Might he see something that suggests the idea? If so, what might that be?

(Enter CLOWN.*)*

A new character enters, and we move into the second section of the scene. What do you imagine the intentional action might be for the step in the story where the two knights are entertained by the clown? Is this a scene where two knights vie for the attention of a popular entertainer? Could it be a scene where Feste enlists the two drunks to raise a ruckus that will embarrass Malvolio; Feste is a man with revenge on his mind as well. Other ideas?

What new given circumstances apply? The Clown enters; from where? From his bed, perhaps? (Picture Feste in this circumstance. What do you suppose a clown wears to bed?) From the wine cellar?

(Toby has just called for wine.) If so, how much might Feste have drunk? Or you might remember that Feste promised Olivia in an earlier scene that "the fool will look after the madman." Might Feste have been here, watching over his charge, all the time?

What could your answers to these questions suggest about changes in pace and rhythm for the events we're about to see?

SIR ANDREW

Here comes the fool, i' faith.

What sort of event might reveal the clown to the sots? Could it startle Andrew? Or could your Andrew slowly come to realize the very, very obvious? Imagine, in detail, a way to time the discovery of the clown.

CLOWN

How now, my hearts? Did you never see the picture of we three?

Here, a look at the footnotes will tell you that you are dealing with another historical "in-joke;" a popular comic picture of Shakespeare's day showed two donkeys looking out at the viewer, suggesting by the title "We Three" that the viewer was an ass.

Will you have Feste accept the role of the third ass for himself? Toby seems to think so:

SIR TOBY

Welcome, ass.

But not too many members of your audience will know about this antique gag. What is important is that we improvise a dramatic *use* for this joke. What is Feste trying to accomplish by telling it? And how could he make that joke strike their ears so that intention is clear?

All of a sudden, Sir Toby has someone else to occupy his attention. How might he feel about that? Might the rhythm and pace of his responses to Sir Andrew's torpor change as he reacts to the razzle-dazzle of Feste's performance? How could such a contrast in tempi articulate the change in Toby's hopes and intentions for this section of the scene?

SIR TOBY (Continued)
Now let's have a catch.

A catch is a kind of group song, usually bawdy, that is arranged for a number of voices in canon. The fun of this kind of singing is that the lyrics, when re-arranged by the rhythm of the overlapping lines, produce rowdy double meanings.

Why might your Sir Toby want to introduce this sort of sprightly music to the scene? Could he hope that this new rhythm will wake Sir Andrew up for another round of drinking perhaps? Or might this be the moment he chooses to initiate his attack on Malvolio?

But Sir Andrew would rather talk than sing:

SIR ANDREW
By my troth, the fool has an excellent breast. I had rather
than forty shillings I had such a leg; and so sweet a breath
to sing as the fool has. In sooth, thou wast in very
gracious fooling last night when thou spokest of Pigrogromitus, of the Vapians passing the equinoctial of Queubus;
'twas very good, i' faith. I sent thee sixpence for thy
leman. Hadst it?

How is it that a man who has spent the entire night eating and drinking suddenly comes out with the longest speech of his role at this particular moment? What is Sir Andrew up to, and how might the rhythm of his speaking reveal that story?

For example, if Andrew were trying to impress Feste with his own verbal facility, we might hear Andrew wade through a phrase like "Pigrogromitus, of the Vapians passing the equinoctial of Queubus" with the deliberate regularity of a man trying to avoid tripping over his own tongue. Or if Andrew were trying to keep Sir Toby's attention for himself, he might speak with the jumpy interrupting cadence of a man who is breaking into Feste's preparation of a catch. Perhaps Andrew's drinking renders him incapable of reporting what Feste actually did say the night before, but he slurs away anyway, oblivious of his own mistakes.

Whatever your choice, Feste, the professional entertainer, will use Andrew's rhythm against him as he ridicules him in kind:

CLOWN

I did impetticos thy gratillity; for Malvolio's nose is no
whipstock. My lady has a white hand, and the Myrmidons are
no bottle-ale houses.

What is the effect of Feste's response? Does your Andrew get it?
What are the ways Andrew might time his next line?:

SIR ANDREW

Excellent! Why, this is the best fooling, when all is done.
Now, a song.

SIR TOBY

Come on; there is sixpence for you: let's have a song.

Why does Andrew agree to a song at this point rather than before his long speech? Why has Andrew obstructed Sir Toby's catch
up until now? What might Andrew believe he has accomplished by
his interruptions? How might the rhythms of the Andrew–Feste exchange tell the story of that accomplishment?

SIR ANDREW

There's a testril of me, too: If one knight give a—

Here's a rhythm interrupted; Feste breaks off Andrew's speech
about paying his share of Feste's fee. Could there be a discovery here?
Of what? By whom?

CLOWN

Would you have a love-song, or a song of good life?

What kind of music will they choose? Why will they choose it?

SIR TOBY

A love-song, a love-song.

SIR ANDREW

Ay, ay; I care not for good life.

How do you imagine Toby and Andrew settling in for Feste's performance? How much, and what kind of time might they occupy as
they prepare themselves to listen? Might they be impatient for the
singing to begin? Are they deliberate about making themselves comfortable for a sweet and nostalgic ballad? Might they stumble over
each other in their drink?

CLOWN

(Singing.)

O, mistress mine, where are you roaming?
O, stay and hear; your true love's coming,
    That can sing both high and low:
Trip no further, pretty sweeting;
    Journeys end in lovers' meeting
        Every wise man's son doth know.

Here we have music literally, and, if original music doesn't come to mind, tradition has passed down a number of tunes to choose from. What sort of music do you imagine for this scene?

To start your thinking, here is John Barton on the subject:

A word about songs. I always think they're a terrible trap in Shakespeare. It's so easy during an exquisite song for the action of the play to get becalmed and for the story to stop moving. I believe that a Shakespearean song or piece of music must always be treated as part of the action of a scene. . . . So, what does the song *do* here?[42]

Barton's suggestion is that we define the song by looking at the effect the song might have on the listening characters, an effect that becomes part of the story because the song impels those characters to act in a way that advances the action of the play. Taking his suggestion, how might the music of this song move the story of this scene ahead? What effects of Feste's singing can you imagine from the responses Shakespeare gives the listeners?

Once you choose the results of the singing you need, you can imagine your way back to the kind of music, and rhythm, that would be most likely to produce those results.

SIR ANDREW

Excellent good, i'faith.

SIR TOBY

Good, good.

Are they breaking in on Feste's song, disrupting its flow? Or might they speak as though they were swept away by the song, commenting in a way that supports the rhythm of the music?

CLOWN

(Singing.)

What is love? 'tis not hereafter;
Present mirth hath present laughter;

What's to come is still unsure:
In delay there lies no plenty;
Then come kiss me, sweet and twenty,
    Youth's a stuff will not endure.

SIR ANDREW

A mellifluous voice, as I am a true knight.

SIR TOBY

A contagious breath.

SIR ANDREW

Very sweet and contagious, i'faith.

What in the music makes Feste's singing "contagious?" Do the hearers hum along? (They certainly join in on Feste's next performance.)

Now Sir Toby decides that he has had enough of this first kind of music. What discovery might account for this change?

He starts with a joke:

SIR TOBY

To hear by the nose, it is dulcet in contagion.

How will this vulgar joke—that it is the smell of the clown's breath, not his music, which is sweet—change the rhythm of Toby's behavior? He's about to "rouse the night-owl." What might his immediate intention, and his new rhythm, be for doing so?

SIR TOBY   (Continued)

But shall we make the welkin dance indeed? Shall we rouse
the night-owl in a catch that will draw three souls out of
one weaver? Shall we do that?

This time, Toby will get his way:

SIR ANDREW

An you love me, let's do't:

Why, now, might Andrew suddenly want to wake up the house with boisterous singing? Has a new idea finally penetrated his besotted thoughts? Have Feste's antics finally brought him around to a wakeful pace? Is this the moment when he discovers Toby's purpose?

And while we're considering music in the scene, can you imagine musical instruments as well as voices at work? A first thought might be that Feste, the performer, comes equipped with a lute. Later, people talk of pipes and tabors (drums). Barton's 1970 production of the play had the inspired notion of having Sir Andrew whip out a bagpipe as Toby began his catch.[43] Imagine the caterwauling *that* would make.

SIR ANDREW   (Continued)
I am a dog at a catch.

CLOWN
By'r lady, sir, and some dogs will catch well.

SIR ANDREW
Most certain: let our catch be, *Thou knave.*

CLOWN
Hold thy peace, thou knave, knight? I shall be constrained in't to call thee knave, knight.

SIR ANDREW
'Tis not the first time I have constrained one to call me knave. Begin, fool; it begins *Hold thy peace.*

CLOWN
I shall never begin if I hold my peace.

SIR ANDREW
Good, i'faith! Come, begin.

Andrew can't wait to get started; it's Feste who delays the start of the song with teasing interruptions and jokes. Why? What is each character's purpose in this tantalizing incident? What might Sir Toby be trying to do while this exchange is taking place? And how might each character use the rhythm of their speech and action to achieve what they want?

(They sing a catch.)

Here, again, the text leaves the specific musical character of the song to your imagination. We do have a title, "Hold Thy Peace," to work with. There is a historical lyric for this song available:

Hold thy peace, thou knave,
And I prithee hold thy peace.[44]

It's a nicely ironic lyric to improvise on—a song asking someone to be quiet as the singers go about the business of making enough noise to wake up the whole household in the dead of night. And some performers have been known to add to that irony, choosing to underline Malvolio's puritanical hypocrisy by making bawdy puns on the words "peace" and "piece."

Still, the action of this incident of singing remains open to improvisation. Is it a contest between the revellers, to see which one can sing loudest? Fastest? With the most elaborate rhythms or choreography? Do they *want* to get Malvolio up? Might one of them want the other two to be blamed for waking Malvolio? Other suggestions?

Whatever story and rhythm you improvise for the song, it must plausibly provoke the beginning of the next section of the scene, which starts when Maria rushes out and says:

MARIA
What a caterwauling do you keep here!

Again, first imagine the intentions provoking the action: Maria is telling the singers to stop their noise before they get into trouble. What sort of trouble do you imagine she might fear? How much time do you suppose she thinks she has? Is she afraid for the singers? Might she think that they were funny? Might she know that Malvolio is right behind her? Could her own position in the house be on the line? Maria is going to end the play as Sir Toby's wife. What might that suggest about the urgency of the present situation in Maria's mind?

Imagine the rest of the circumstances: Where do you think Maria has come from? Has she been where she can fetch the "stoop of wine" Toby called for? Might she be rising from her bed? When might she have first heard the knights? How could she have been occupied in the time between that moment and now?

How might each of these choices sound in the pace and rhythm of her behavior as she says:

MARIA   (Continued)
If my lady have not called up her steward, Malvolio, and bid him turn you out of doors, never trust me.

She is not going to succeed. Toby's noise rises unabated:

SIR TOBY

My Lady's a Cataian, we are politicians; Malvolio's a Peg-a-Ramsay, and *Three merry men are we.*

What might Toby be intending to accomplish? Could he be trying to provoke a final show-down with Malvolio, shouting to bring him out? Might he be trying to give courage to his daunted followers for the show-down to come? Or could Toby be trying to impress Maria with his challenge? Each intention could suggest a different rhythm.

Toby then moves on to the substance of his argument:

SIR TOBY   (Continued)

Am I not consanguineous? Am I not of her blood? Tilly-valley, Lady!

(Singing.)

There dwelt a man in Babylon, lady, lady.

Will you have him singing alone? Who might join Toby in his defiance of Malvolio's authority? How might that sound?

Again, scholars have found some lyrics from Shakespeare's day that the playwright probably had in mind when he wrote short sections of song for Toby and the others to sing. They are scraps of song from George Peele's *Old Wives' Tale* (1595):

Three merry men, and three merry men
    And three merry men be we:
I in the wood, and thou on the ground
    And Jack sleeps in the tree.

and:

There dwelt a man in Babylon
Of reputation great by fame:
He took a wife, a fair woman,
Suzanna she was called by name.
A woman fair and virtuous
Lady, lady . . .[45]

How could you imagine Toby might use these or other musical devices to get what he wants, to draw Malvolio out to fight? He can sing; could he also shout? Dance? Drum on garbage cans?

CLOWN

Beshrew me, the knight's in admirable fooling.

SIR ANDREW

Ay, he does well enough if he be disposed, and so do I too:
he does it with a better grace, but I do it more natural.

SIR TOBY
O, the twelfth day of December,—

MARIA
For the love o' God, peace.

There are at least three intentions at work in this exchange. Feste and Andrew are engaged in some sort of critical assessment of Toby's performance; what sort? What reason might each have in offering their judgments to each other? Will you have them join Sir Toby to prove their point? Sir Toby is singing away. How might you imagine he is carrying on? Is he making progress in his intentions at this point? And Maria is trying to win some "peace." What might be on her agenda at this moment? And how can you imagine articulating these contrasting intentions in contrasting rhythms of behavior?

This counterpoint of rhythms is reaching a climax of foolery. How do you imagine it growing in intensity until the moment when:

(Enter MALVOLIO.)

How do you imagine the rhythms of Malvolio's entrance? Here's an example: Laurence Olivier had him appear in his nightshirt and cap with his pants hurriedly pulled up to cover his legs. He wore his chain of office as if he slept in it or as if it were the very first thing he grabbed for as he rose from his bed. That's one story—a man trying to impress people with his dignity and authority even as he clutches at his pants to keep them from falling down.[46]

What other stories occur to you for this moment? How else might Malvolio rise from his bed (or from some other place, perhaps? Where?), and what would lead him to gird his loins to meet his nemesis, Toby? Might he be entering as if he were trying to catch housebreakers in the act? Might he appear, in full regalia, using a rhythm of state to intimidate his underlings into submission? Could he come on with the zealous rhythm of a puritan scold, warning these lost souls of the exile that awaits them?:

MALVOLIO
My masters, are you mad? or what are you? Have you no wit, manners, nor honesty, but to gabble like tinkers at this

time of night? Do ye make an ale-house of my lady's house,
that ye squeak out your coziers' catches without any mitiga-
tion or remorse of voice? Is there no respect of place,
persons, nor time, in you?

Might your Malvolio be trying to shout down the riotous singers?
Or might you have his solemn appearance strike everyone silent, giving him time to eye them carefully and speak in the quiet and regular rhythm of weighty authority? Might he pause after every question,
hoping to make miscreants squirm in guilt? Could he rush from accusation to accusation, cutting off all protests of innocence before
anybody else can say a word?

What sorts of responses do you imagine he could receive? Andrew, for example, has no more lines until Malvolio leaves the stage;
how might he receive this tongue lashing? Is he cowed into silence?
Might he be trying to deal with the problem of being caught at night
in his lady's house uninvited? Or could he be about to protest when
Toby takes the field for himself:

SIR TOBY
We did keep time, sir, in our catches. Sneck up!

The two principal combatants of the scene face off: Both Toby and
Malvolio claim precedence in Olivia's house, Toby because he is
Olivia's uncle, and Malvolio because he believes that his virtue and
sagacity deserve no less. Yet perhaps neither are at their best. Toby
has been drinking all night, and Malvolio could be just up out of bed,
facing a quartet of people, each of whom has reason to wish to see him
embarrassed, or worse.

MALVOLIO
Sir Toby, I must be round with you.

When Malvolio speaks he uses the stern vocabulary of cold and
condescending courtesy. But will you have him use that rhythm? He
might speak in the regular cadence of a man who fully expects to be
obeyed. He might also use the darting and tentative speech of a man
who is risking everything as he dares to chastise a knight, and a
member of his mistress' family. Which makes the most sense to you?
What are the consequences of each choice? Try them out:

MALVOLIO   (Continued)

My lady bade me tell you that though she harbours you as her
kinsman she's nothing allied to your disorders. If you can
separate yourself and your misdemeanours, you are welcome to
the house; if not, an it would please you to take leave of
her, she is very willing to bid you farewell.

Will your Malvolio be telling the truth here? Might he have literally gone to Olivia and received these instructions? Or could he be
making up these conditions on the spot? Could he be bluffing? Would
he know it? How might each possibility determine the rhythm of his
behavior?

What effect will your choice of rhythm have on Malvolio's listeners? Might they be struck dumb at this terrible threat? Will Toby's
song be the thing to restore their courage? Or could they see through
the steward's pretension and explode with laughter as Toby pounces
on Malvolio's last word to make a funny song out of it?

SIR TOBY

Farewell, dear heart, since I must needs be gone.

Might Maria still fear Malvolio's authority in the house? Could
she be afraid for Sir Toby, on whom she's pinned her hopes? Or could
she be beginning to join the rebellion and the fun? How could her behavior indicate her intention as she says:

MARIA

Nay, good Sir Toby.

Feste is about to join in; does his singing support Toby's performance? Could your Feste give Toby a new idea for foolery as he
sings? How?

CLOWN

His eyes do show his days are almost done.

For example, could Feste and Toby break into some sort of improvised opera, using the words of an old song as if it were a coarse
recitativo? Might it be like a music hall routine? How could your characters use their singing to call Malvolio's bluff?

MALVOLIO

Is't even so?

To whom could Malvolio be speaking? Might he be trying to interrupt the singers before they get entirely out of hand? Might Malvolio intend this as a threat? To Maria? To Andrew? We know it has no effect on the singers themselves. What other effect might Malvolio be after?

SIR TOBY

But I will never die.

CLOWN

Sir Toby, there you lie.

For this quick and mordant interjection, Feste chooses not to sing, but to improvise a remark that is in perfect rhyme and meter with Toby's sung verse. What purpose might Feste have in reminding Toby of his fallibility and mortality at this moment?

MALVOLIO

This is much credit to you.

Credit to whom? Who can you imagine might be the next candidate for blame from Malvolio's frustrated imagination? How might that change of target change Malvolio's behavior?

SIR TOBY

Shall I bid him go?

CLOWN

What an if you do?

Bid who go? Might Sir Toby be proposing an ejection of Malvolio? Or could he be aping Malvolio, threatening to send someone else away?

SIR TOBY

Shall I bid him go and spare not?

CLOWN

O no, no, no, no, you dare not.

What about those four "no's"? Might Feste be daring Toby to finish Malvolio off in some way? Could he be singing in mock horror at

Toby's *lèse majesté*? Could he pause to consider Toby's odds of success between each "no"?

SIR TOBY

Out o' tune? sir, ye lie.—

Toby abruptly ends the musical performance with this blunt remark. How might it end? Could Toby and Feste reach a satisfying musical finish, amusing their hearers at Malvolio's expense? Might Toby have had enough, suddenly breaking off the fun and interrupting the singing to crush the impudent steward with plain speech? The rhythm of the action sharply changes at this moment in the text, but it remains for you to choose from what to what?

SIR TOBY (Continued)

Art any more than a steward? Dost thou think, because thou art virtuous, there shall be no more cakes and ale?

And Feste, again, is quick to join in; but how?

CLOWN

Yes, by Saint Anne; and ginger shall be hot i' the mouth, too.

SIR TOBY

Thou'rt in the right.—Go, sir, rub your chain with crumbs: A stoop of wine, Maria!

How might Toby call for his glass? Could this cry for more wine be the climax of his victory over Malvolio, cheering on cowering followers? Might it be Toby's way of showing Malvolio who has the real authority over the servants in this house? Might he be trying to put Malvolio in his place, calling for the wine he failed to get earlier in the scene because the interferring steward tried to break up his betters' party?

This call for drink puts Maria in an awkward position between the man she loves and the man she fears. How might she respond to Toby's request? And how might that response provoke Malvolio to say:

MALVOLIO

Mistress Mary, if you prized my lady's favour at anything more than contempt, you would not give means for this uncivil rule: she shall know of it by this hand.

(Exit.)

MARIA

Go shake your ears.

One of the most interesting stories to follow in this scene is the tale of Maria's conversion. It is Maria who undergoes a fundamental change. She enters the stage warning Toby and trying to get him to conform to Malvolio's authority. She ends the scene hatching the plot that will bring Malvolio to humiliation within the household and confinement in a madhouse. By this point in the text, she has made her decision. She chooses to join Sir Toby in his defiance of Malvolio. But at what earlier moment in the scene will you have her make the discovery that leads to this choice? What specific incident might tip the balance for her? Imagine a rhythm of action for the specific incidents you need to articulate the story of Maria's discoveries and decision to join Toby's rebellion.

When he exits, where might Malvolio choose to go? Could he be going to wake up Olivia and complain about Toby? (Or about Maria, as he threatens?) Could he go back to his room to plot a suitable revenge? In John Guilgud's production, Olivier raised his hand to swear revenge, "by this hand," and lost his pants in the process, leaving the stage in rhythmic confusion, to everybody's hilarious celebration.[47] Donald Sinden, however, describes his choices for Malvolio's exit this way:

> Sir Toby and Feste are untamed. Right, then—I will break it up by removing their supplies . . . I take the glass U and behind the table where I find that they have *all* been using glass goblets—not only that, but also one of my Lady's best decanters and a silver tray and a silver candelabra on which are burning *three* candles. They cost a great deal of money and I am responsible for the household accounts! This will never happen again! I pick up the tray and all its contents. Suddenly I hear Sir Toby at my L saying, "Art any more than a steward?" My lips tighten, my eyes narrow (stop before you go too far). "Rub your chain with crumbs," he says, and "A stoop of wine, Maria." My chance. He cannot, he shall not, involve *my* servants. My head lashes around to Maria, who is about to follow Sir Toby's request. "Mistress Mary" is spoken quietly but menacingly; there is no doubt about it meaning "stand still." "She shall know of it" (tell-tale) "by this hand." A final sneer at them all—particularly Sir Toby, for my last remarks were as much for his benefit as Maria's; my head erect, tray held carefully, sharp R turn I march off R (An imperceptible half step back wards before L, R, L, R).[48]

It's useful to compare these two improvisations for this moment: Guilgud and Olivier chose, among lots of other effective ideas, a rhythm of hysterical and humiliated confusion; Malvolio was trying to escape the scene as his pants fell down. Sinden's purposeful march rhythm with his rescued tray—undercut with a hitch-step—tells a very different story.

When Malvolio leaves the stage, a new section of the scene begins—the moment of Maria's conspiracy. Maria has to convert Sir Toby's dangerous impulses to more effective and safer schemes. She has to meet his thoughtless enthusiasm with deliberate argument. What rhythms might articulate that story?

The section begins with the revellers' reaction to Malvolio's exit. Do you imagine an explosion of wild cheering and laughter? Might there be a snorting secret celebration, muffled so as not to disturb Olivia, or perhaps there's a moment of silent fear once they realize the risk they have just run?

Whatever event you choose, it must accomplish one thing—plausibly bring Sir Andrew's voice back into the scene after a long period of silence.

SIR ANDREW
'Twere as good a deed as to drink when a man's a-hungry, to
challenge him to the field, and then to break promise with
him and make a fool of him.

What intention can you imagine might impel Andrew to say this speech? Could this be the speech of a man who has been trying to hide away until Malvolio has been defeated by others, then jumping in, trying to catch up, to get credit for participation in the fight he was too cowardly to join? Or might this dim scheme, a contribution Andrew has been struggling to articulate throughout the whole confrontation, just now have come into focus in his febrile mind? Or might he be speaking in the rhythm of a man who is trying to give his friends heart with a new scheme to replace the one that has landed them in trouble?

Sir Toby seems to pounce on the suggestion:

SIR TOBY
Do't, knight; I'll write thee a challenge; or I'll deliver
thy indignation to him by word of mouth.

How do you imagine hearing, and seeing, Sir Toby make this proposal? It's an idea he must have some enthusiasm for; he'll refer to it again in the false duel he'll set up between Sir Andrew and Viola later in the play.

At any rate, it must establish a rhythm that suggests impatience, a rhythm Maria can plausibly break up with her counter proposal:

> MARIA
> Sweet Sir Toby, be patient for tonight; since the youth of
> the count's was to-day with my lady she is much out of
> quiet. For Monsieur Malvolio, let me alone with him: if I
> do not gull him into a nayword, and make him a common
> recreation, do not think I have wit enough to lie straight
> in my bed. I know I can do it.

With this speech Maria takes charge. How will you have her accomplish this? When might she have hatched her plan? Could the idea be clear in her mind before she speaks, so she is informing the men of a fully developed plot? Or could she be improvising a plan on the spot to keep Toby from hurting himself even more in Olivia's eyes? These choices each suggest distinct rhythms of behavior and speech.

When, in the course of her speech, might Sir Toby and Sir Andrew each decide to "be patient for to-night"? Will your Maria sense their change of mind? How? Try to imagine the rhythms of behavior that might articulate their conversion from itching to charge out and pick a fight to deciding to listen to Maria and hear her good idea.

> SIR TOBY
> Possess, possess us; tell us something of him.

Maria has their attention. What's the next rhythm you might hear for the hatching of a conspiracy?

> MARIA
> Marry, sir, sometimes he is a kind of Puritan.

Looking ahead, Maria seems to be setting up an argument that Malvolio is not a puritan at all, but a hypocrite who hides lubricous fantasies under a mask of righteousness. However, she doesn't get the chance to finish her thought. Sir Andrew jumps in with:

> SIR ANDREW
> O, if I thought that, I'd beat him like a dog.

SIR TOBY

What, for being like a Puritan? thy exquisite reason, dear
knight?

SIR ANDREW

I have no exquisite reason for't, but I have reason good
enough.

This has the effect of compelling Maria to speak to get the gentlemen's
attention (and tempo) back on track:

MARIA

The devil a Puritan that he is, or anything constantly but a
time pleaser: an affection'd ass that cons state without
book and utters it by great swarths;

How could Maria be using and shaping this time once she has
won the men's attention? Might she be entertaining the men to distract them from further trouble? Is she selling her idea to skeptics?
Could she be trying to offer a gift to a lover ("Sweet Sir Toby")?

MARIA   (Continued)

the best persuaded of himself, so crammed, as he thinks,
with excellencies, that it is his ground of faith that all
that look on him love him;

And now, Maria will change subject from her background description of Malvolio to the details of her plan. What changes of rhythm
of speaking and acting might best articulate her thoughts as she reveals her idea?

MARIA   (Continued)

and on that vice in him will my revenge find notable cause
to work.

SIR TOBY

What wilt thou do?

Do you imagine a Sir Toby who speaks these words in the rhythm
of a man anxious to get to the details of the fun? Or that of a man surprised that anybody could top his famous victory over the detested
Malvolio? Or of a man trying, through the haze of too much alcohol, to
follow the faster thinking of someone who still has her wits about her?

MARIA

I will drop in his way some obscure epistles of love;
wherein, by the colour of his beard, the shape of his leg,
the manner of his gait, the expressure of his eye, fore-
head, and complexion, he shall find himself most feelingly
personated.

Might you hear the rhythm of a new idea occurring to her as she says:

MARIA   (Continued)

I can write very like my lady, your niece; on a forgotten
matter we can hardly make distinction of our hands.

Or is she revealing the secret she's been holding back, like a trump
card, for its greatest effect?

In either case, this is the detail that wins Sir Toby over. How do
you imagine he sounds as he says:

SIR TOBY

Excellent! I smell a device.

SIR ANDREW

I haven't in my nose too.

Does he? When might Sir Andrew catch on, really? Now? Perhaps. But could he also be simply trying not to be left out, or left behind, as Toby and Maria hatch their conspiracies? Or could he imagine that he is competing with Sir Toby for Maria's appreciation and
attention?

How might your Sir Toby receive Sir Andrew's contribution at
this point?

SIR TOBY

He shall think, by the letters that thou wilt drop, that
they are come from thy niece, and that she is in love with
him.

Do you imagine a Sir Toby who is sorting out Maria's plan in his own
mind? Or one who is spelling out the plan for a dull witted Sir Andrew's instruction? Or is the light bulb of discovery just flashing on in
his head? Might he be asking Maria if he's guessed her idea correctly?

Whatever you choose, it is Maria who settles the matter:

MARIA

My purpose is, indeed, a horse of that colour.

But need it be Maria who first gets the idea that Malvolio be gulled sexually as well as socially? Toby's the first one to offer this possibility. Can you imagine a plausible version of this story where Maria gets as many ideas from Toby as he gets from her? If so, how might the rhythms of those moments of mutual invention sound?

Andrew now chimes in with his own joke:

SIR ANDREW

And your horse now would make him an ass.

But his way of making his contribution prompts Maria to call him, in turn, an ass:

MARIA

Ass, I doubt not.

So imagine how Andrew could say his line to provoke this response. And how might the rhythm of her reply convey a meaning that might logically lead Andrew to accept Maria's insult with good humor? (If that's what you imagine him doing.)

SIR ANDREW

O 'twill be admirable.

MARIA

Sport royal, I warrent you. I know my physic will work with
him. I will plant you two, and let the fool make a third,
where he shall find the letter; observe his construction of
it. For this night, to bed, and dream on the event.

(Exit.)

Maria, having disposed of distractions and interruptions, is now in charge. Sir Toby acknowledges her successful achievement by giving her the title of a famous warrior-queen:

SIR TOBY

Good-night, Penthesilea.

So might you have her leave with the rhythm of someone who has just issued orders to her troops?

With Maria's exit, we come into the final section of the scene.

Who's left? What has become of Feste? In some productions, he leaves with Malvolio; in others, he follows Maria into the house, and in others, he stays, silent, to carry out Olivia's orders that he "look after" Sir Toby. Will you have him there? Has he heard that he's to be part of the letter plot? (In the event, the text indicates that it's not Feste but Fabian who makes the third.) If so, what might he be trying to accomplish? How might he silently contribute to the rhythm of the action?

The speakers are Sir Toby and Sir Andrew, the two characters who began the scene. Might they return to old intentions and rhythms, Sir Toby trying to arouse Sir Andrew to win more money for more drink, and Sir Andrew trying to find a comfortable place to sleep? Perhaps. Or could the confrontation with Malvolio and the hatching of the plot have changed their given circumstances, filling their heads with new thoughts, and hence, a new rhythm?

SIR ANDREW

Before me, she's a good wench.

SIR TOBY

She's a beagle true bred, and one that adores me. What o' that?

Why does your Sir Toby make light of Maria's affection for him? What thought might inform the question, "What o' that?" Might Toby regret that his station in life prevents him from responding, as he wishes he could, to the love of a servant? Might he simply be a man taking advantage of the girl's adoration? Could he believe that he is unworthy of such a brilliant woman, so he'd better protect himself from his own feelings for her? How might your sense of Toby's thinking cause him to speak and act at this moment?

SIR ANDREW

I was adored once, too.

This line is a suggestive one as well. Is it true? Was this fool *ever* adored? By whom? Might Sir Andrew be defending his own ego against Sir Toby's easy assumption of Maria's adoration? Might he be lost in nostalgia for a lost love? Could he be demanding that Sir Toby make good on his promise to introduce him to Olivia now that Malvolio is about to be removed?

How might that intention provoke the next change of subject:

SIR TOBY
Let's to bed, knight.

But then something must happen to make Sir Toby think of a new pursuit—a new intention that might require a new rhythm. What specific event or thought might make your Sir Toby think of his financial situation?

SIR TOBY   (Continued)
—Thou hadst need send for more money.

SIR ANDREW
If I cannot recover your niece, I am a foul way out.

SIR TOBY
Send for money, knight; if thou hast her not i' the end,
call me Cut.

SIR ANDREW
If I do not, never trust me; take it how you will.

In one theatrical tradition, going back to the Kembles, the mention of money is the one thing that manages to wake Andrew. He hectors Toby off the stage, pursuing him, saying over and over again, "Cut! Cut! Cut!"[49] But perhaps your Sir Andrew's mind is working differently. Maybe his liquor has finally gotten the better of him and sent him looking for a dark corner where he can curl up and finally go to sleep. If so, the rhythm closing this scene will be different from the chase the Kembles invented.

SIR TOBY   (Continued)
Come, come; I'll go burn some sack; 'tis too late to go to
bed now.

What time of night might it have become? Why might Toby mention the hour? A bell? The sound of Andrew's heavy breathing? Dawn lighting up the sky? Or the fact that Andrew is chasing him to get some money back?

SIR TOBY   (Continued)
Come knight; come knight.

(Exeunt.)

Where do you suppose each of them might be going? Or failing to go? What is the rate and the rhythm of their departure? Or of their staying?

As you answer these questions and make your particular choices of rhythm for scene, I hope you can begin to see how time, applied in its musical sense, can suggest a specific understanding of what's going on in the play. Since plays consume time, they have to organize the time they use up. If the audience's time is broken up into short bursts of action, their understanding and response to what they are watching will be different than if that same time were filled by performers offering a slow succession of sustained incidents. Therefore, choosing particular rhythmic patterns for the action is part of choosing what the audience will come to understand as they watch the play. Learning to take advantage of the narrative possibilities of rhythm in the theatre is an essential part of any actor's or director's preparation for the stage.

CHAPTER 11

Structure

The original stage direction is "Enter Suffolk with Margaret in his hand" but we altered the order of the scenes here, moving Margaret's first entrance to follow rather than precede the death of Joan of Arc. . . . With Joan of Arc at the stake and dead bodies on the stage, I came on covered in a brown cloak, hungry, a scavenger on the battlefield, like a sewer rat sniffing for the remnants of the picnic that York and Warwick had been eating while Joan was burning.[50]

—PENNY DOWNIE

Sometimes it's helpful to remember the obvious: Shakespeare was a playwright, not a "playwrite." This common misspelling matters. Plays are wrought, they are not, strictly speaking, written. That is, they are built. Plays are crafted by a team of people. It takes all sorts of sensibilities and skills to assemble a complete performance.

Still, the initiator of all this building, the architect, if you will, is the playwright. In writing a text for the stage, Shakespeare was the man who drew up the plans and designed a structure for the yet-to-be-realized piece. He chose the building blocks (incidents of fictional behavior for his audiences to see and hear) and planned an orderly arrangement that made them make sense.

The order in which fictional acts are arranged becomes structurally sound when it, too, contributes to a virtual logic capable of persuading spectators to "suspend their disbelief." If incident A is placed so that it happens at one point in the play, that placement should appear to cause or give specific significance to B when it comes about, which seems, in turn, to lead believably to the occurrence of C, and so on. If each act appears in a designed arrangement of acts that suggests this sort of persuasive dramatic logic, each act can appear to be plausible, and the illusion can succeed. The construction will stand on its own.

Penny Downie's report describes a production that rearranged the events in the *Henry VI* plays, creating a new structure that, from the sound of it, was rather effective. Set aside the ethical questions raised by the director's decision to alter the playwright's original structure. For our purposes, it's enough to note that once the order of the scenes was altered, the nature and the significance of the action was determined in a new way for the character, for the actor, and for the audience. A content for the incident was largely suggested by where it was placed in the succession of events that made up the plot of that play.

The structure of a Shakespearean text is specific and clear, and we will stick to it; still, for the reading actor or director, the dramatic possibilities suggested by the structure of any play remain open to an evocative range of improvisation. There are many choices waiting to be made. So, as you are digging into the dramatic possibilities suggested by the playwright's crafting of language and manipulations of time, ask more actor's questions about the position occupied by each act in the plot. What does the placement of each incident suggest to you about its causes and implications?

Here is a section of a pivotal scene. Consider how its events might be affected by the position they occupy in the chain of events that is *Othello*:

Enter OTHELLO

IAGO (Continued)
　　　　　　　Not poppy, nor mandragora,
Nor all the drowsy syrups of the world,
Shall ever medicine thee to that sweet sleep
Which thou ow'dst yesterday.

OTHELLO
　　　Ha! ha! false to me?

IAGO

Why, how now, general? No more of that.

OTHELLO

Avaunt! be gone! Thou hast set me on the rack.
I swear 'tis better to be much abus'd
Than but to know't a little.

IAGO

How now, my lord?

OTHELLO

What sense had I of her stol'n hours of lust?
I saw't not, thought it not, it harm'd not me.
I slept the next night well, was free and merry;
I found not Cassio's kisses on her lips.
He that is robb'd, not wanting what is stol'n,
Let him not know't and he's not robb'd at all.

IAGO

I am sorry to hear this.

OTHELLO

I had been happy if the general camp,
Pioneers and all, had tasted her sweet body,
So I had nothing known. O, now for ever
Farewell the tranquil mind! farewell content!
Farewell the plumed troops and the big wars
That make ambition virtue! O, farewell!
Farewell the neighing steed, and the shrill trump,
The spirit-stirring drum, th' ear-piercing fife,
The royal banner, and all quality,
Pride, pomp, and circumstance of glorious war!
And, O ye mortal engines, whose wide throats
Th' immortal Jove's great clamor counterfeit,
Farewell! Othello's occupation's gone!

IAGO

Is't possible, my lord?

OTHELLO

Villain, be sure thou prove my love a whore,
Be sure of it! Give me oracular proof:
Or by the worth of man's eternal soul,

Thou hadst been better have been born a dog
Than answer my wak'd wrath.

IAGO

Is't come to this?

OTHELLO

Make me see't; or, at the least, so prove it
That the probation bear no hinge nor loop
To hang a doubt on, or woe upon thy life!

IAGO

My noble lord,—

OTHELLO

If thou dost slander her and torture me,
Never pray more. Abandon all remorse;
On horror's head horrors accumulate;
Do deeds to make heaven weep, all earth amaz'd
For nothing canst thou to damnation add
Greater than that.

IAGO

O grace! O heaven defend me!
Are you a man? Have you soul or sense?
God be wi' you! Take mine office. O wretched fool!
That liv'st to make thine honesty a vice.
O monstrous world! Take note, take note, O world,
To be direct and honest is not safe.
I thank you for this profit, and from hence
I'll love no friend, sith love breeds such offense.

OTHELLO

Nay, stay. Thou shouldst be honest.

IAGO

I should be wise, for honesty's a fool,
And loses what it works for.

OTHELLO

By the world,
I think my wife be honest and think she is not;
I think that thou art just and think thou art not.
I'll have some proof. Her name, that was as fresh

As Dian's visage, is now begrim'd and black
As mine own face. If there be cords or knives,
Poison or fire or suffocating streams,
I'll not endure it. Would I were satisfied!

IAGO

I see, sir, you are eaten up with passion.
I do repent me that I put it to you.
You would be satisfied?

OTHELLO

Would? Nay, I will!

IAGO

And may; but how? How satisfied, my lord?
Would you, the supervisor, grossly gape on,
Behold her topp'd?

OTHELLO

Death and damnation! O!

IAGO

It were a tedious difficulty, I think,
To bring them to that prospect. Damn them then,
If ever mortal eyes do see them bolster
More than their own. What then? how then?
What shall I say? Where's satisfaction?
It is impossible you should see this,
Were they as prime as goats, as hot as monkeys,
As salt as wolves in pride, and fools as gross
As ignorance made drunk. But yet, I say,
If imputation, and strong circumstances,
Which lead directly to the door of truth,
Will give you satisfaction, you may have't.

OTHELLO

Give me a living reason she's disloyal.

IAGO

I do not like the office;
But sith I am entered in this cause so far
(Prick'd to't by foolish honesty and love),
I will go on. I lay with Cassio lately;
And, being troubled with a raging tooth,

I could not sleep.
There are a kind of men so loose of soul
That in their sleeps will mutter their affairs.
One of this kind is Cassio.
In sleep I heard him say, 'Sweet Desdemona,
Let us be wary, let us hide our loves!'
And then, sir, would he gripe and wring my hand,
Cry out 'Sweet creature!' and then kiss me hard,
As if he pluck'd up kisses by the roots
That grew upon my lips, then laid his leg
Over my thigh, and sigh'd, and kiss'd, and then
Cried, 'Cursed fate, that gave thee to the Moor!'

OTHELLO

O monstrous! monstrous!

IAGO

Nay, this was but his dream.

OTHELLO

But this denoted a foregone conclusion.

IAGO

'Tis a shrewd doubt, though it be but a dream;
And this may help to thicken other proofs
That do demonstrate thinly.

OTHELLO

I'll tear her all to pieces!

IAGO

Nay, but be wise. Yet we see nothing done;
She may be honest yet. Tell me but this:
Have you not sometimes seen a handkerchief
Spotted with strawberries in your wife's hand?

OTHELLO

I gave her such a one. 'Twas my first gift.

IAGO

I know not that; but such a handkerchief
(I am sure it was your wife's) did I to-day
See Cassio wipe his beard with.

OTHELLO

If it be that,—

IAGO

If it be that, or any that was hers,
It speaks against her with the other proofs.

OTHELLO

O that the slave had forty thousand lives!
One is too poor, too weak, for my revenge.
Now do I see 'tis true. Look here, Iago;
All my fond love thus do I blow to heaven.

(Hisses contemptuously.)

'Tis gone.
Arise black vengeance, from thy hollow cell!
Yield up, O love, thy crown and hearted throne
To tyrannous hate. Swell, bosom, with thy fraught,
For 'tis of aspics' tongues!

IAGO

Pray, be content.

OTHELLO

O blood! Iago, blood!

IAGO

Patience, I say. Your mind, perhaps, may change.

OTHELLO

Never Iago. Like to the Pontic sea,
Whose icy current and compulsive course
Ne'er feels retiring ebb, but keeps due on
To the Propontio and the Hellespont,
Even so my bloody thoughts, with violent pace,
Shall ne'er look back, ne'er ebb to humble love,
Till that a capable and wide revenge
Swallow them up.

(He kneels.)

Now, by yond marble heaven,
In the due reverence of a sacred vow
I here engage my words.

IAGO

                    Do not rise yet.
Witness, you ever burning lights above!
You elements that clip us round about!
Witness that here Iago doth give up
The execution of his wit, hands, heart,
To wrong'd Othello's service! Let him command,
And to obey shall be in me remorse,
What bloody work soever.

(They rise.)

OTHELLO

                    I greet thy love,
Not with vain thanks, but with acceptance bounteous,
And will upon the instant put thee to't.
Within these three days let me hear thee say
That Cassio's not alive.

IAGO

My friend is dead; 'tis done as you request.
But let her live.

OTHELLO

          Damn her, lewd minx! O, damn her!
Come, go with me apart. I will withdraw   .
To furnish me with some swift means of death
For the fair devil. Now art thou my lieutenant.

IAGO

I am your own for ever.

(Exeunt.)

This exchange between Iago and Othello is, of course, the last part
of a larger scene, Act III, Scene iii. Each incident that occurs between
them here happens in the context of the earlier events of that scene.
What we want to explore is how the location of each act in that order
of incidents might suggest a range of plausible meanings for each of
these acts.

As before, begin by breaking the whole scene into its steps of physical action, the events the audience will see and hear. Your list might turn out to look something like this:

Scene 3
[*The Garden of the Citadel*]

I. DESDEMONA, CASSIO, EMELIA
Desdemona and Emelia assure Cassio, who is afraid that his position is lost after his embarrassing failure of responsibility the previous night, that they will speak on his behalf to their husbands.

II. *Enter* OTHELLO and IAGO *Apart*
Cassio, humiliated, excuses himself despite Desdemona's offer to plead his case immediately and openly.

III. *Exit* CASSIO; IAGO and OTHELLO speak *Apart*
Iago tells Othello that Cassio is stealing away "guilty-like."

IV. IAGO, OTHELLO, DESDEMONA, EMELIA
    A. As she promised, Desdemona pleads Cassio's case; she asks Othello to "set a time certain" when Cassio will be recalled; she reminds Othello that it was Cassio who "came a-wooing with him."
    B. Othello agrees to call Cassio back; "I will deny thee nothing."
    C. Desdemona chides Othello; he should recall Cassio for his own "peculiar profit," not just to please her. She teases Othello, saying when she is asking for something for herself, "it shall be full of poise and difficulty / And fearful to be granted."
    D. Othello asks to be left alone.
    E. Desdemona complies; "Whate'er you be, I am obedient."

V. IAGO, OTHELLO
    A. Othello declares his love for Desdemona; "And when I love thee not / Chaos is come again."
    B. Iago asks Othello to tell him the history of his friendship with Cassio.
    C. Othello, saying he trusts Iago as honest, wants to know what Iago suspects. Iago equivocates, saying he should be sure of his suspicions before he articulates them.
    D. Othello demands that Iago tell him his thoughts. Iago hesitates further. Othello says "Ha!"

E. Othello's outburst has the apparent effect of forcing Iago to say, "Beware, my lord, of jealousy."

F. Othello argues that he is above all thoughts of jealousy. He will act on clear evidence, nothing less. "I'll see before I doubt; when I doubt prove: / And, on the proof, there is no more but this: / Away at once with love or jealousy!"

G. Iago then agrees to warn Othello to look to his wife, to "Observe her well with Cassio . . . . In Venice they do let God see the pranks / They dare not show their husbands."

H. Othello thanks Iago.

I. Iago apologizes to Othello for having disturbed him. Othello denies that Iago has bothered his thoughts.

J. Othello then wonders aloud; "And yet, how Nature erring from itself . . . ."

K. Iago interrupts, telling Othello that that's just the point; Desdemona acted unnaturally when she chose Othello rather than suitors "Of her own clime, complexion, and degree." He claims that such a woman must be unpredictable, and may have regretted her choice.

L. Othello orders Iago to get Emelia to observe Desdemona for him.

VI. OTHELLO *Alone*

Othello wonders why he chose to marry, and asks how much more Iago may know.

VII. OTHELLO and IAGO

Iago returns to ask that Othello delay Cassio's reinstatement so that he may discover, from Desdemona's pleading, what their relationship might be. Othello agrees, and reassures Iago that he is trusted.

VIII. OTHELLO *Alone*

A. Othello says that Iago understands human nature better than he.

B. Othello claims that if he proves that Desdemona has been a "haggard," he will dismiss her; "I'd whistle her off and let her down the wind, / To prey at fortune."

C. Othello speculates about reasons why Desdemona might have rejected him—he is black, and does not know the courtly language of white lovers; he is too old for her.

    D. If so, his only relief is to loathe her, he says.

    E. "Oh curse of marriage! / That we can call these delicate crea-tures ours / And not their appetites." Men of authority are always deceived by their wives.

    F. Seeing Desdemona in the distance, he appears to reject these thoughts; "If she is false, O then heaven mocks itself. / I'll not believe it."

IX. OTHELLO, DESDEMONA, EMELIA

    A. Othello excuses himself from an official dinner, complaining of a pain upon his forehead. Desdemona offers to bind it with her handkerchief.

    B. Othello, saying, "your napkin is too little," pushes the hand-kerchief aside and lets it drop, ordering Desdemona to for-get about it.

X. EMILIA *Alone*

Emilia picks up the handkerchief and says she'll have a copy of it made for Iago who asked her to steal it for him.

XI. IAGO, EMELIA

    A. Emelia teases Iago with the handkerchief.

    B. Iago takes the handkerchief from Emelia, refusing to answer her questions about what he plans to do with it. Iago dis-misses Emelia.

XII. IAGO *Alone*

Iago says he will plant the handkerchief in Cassio's lodgings; "trifles light as air / Are to the jealous confirmations strong."

XIII. OTHELLO AND IAGO

    A. Iago, in an aside, celebrates his evident success in disturbing Othello's mind.

    B. Othello tells Iago that his new suspicions of Desdemona have so disturbed his mind that he is no longer capable of fulfill-ing his office: "Farewell the tranquil mind! Farewell content. . . . Othello's occupation's gone!"

    C. Othello orders Iago to "Prove my love a whore," or "woe upon thy life."

    D. Iago claims that, under Othello's governance, "to be honest is not safe."

E. Othello demands that he be "satisfied."

F. Iago asks Othello what will satisfy him; "Would you, the supervisor, grossly gape on, / Behold her topp'd?" Othello can only respond with a curse: "Death and damnation! O!"

G. Iago asks Othello if circumstantial evidence will do: "If imputation, and strong circumstances / Which lead directly to the door of truth / Will give you satisfaction, you may have it."

H. Othello agrees; he will accept circumstantial evidence if it is persuasive. "Give me living reason she's disloyal."

I. Iago tells Othello the story of Cassio lying on him and kissing him as if he were Desdemona.

J. Othello calls the story "monstrous," and swears, "I'll tear her all to pieces."

K. Iago counsels caution.

L. Iago says he saw Cassio wipe his beard with Desdemona's handkerchief earlier that day.

M. Othello responds, "If't be that . . . . Now do I see 'tis true."

N. Othello now claims he is free of love and will be driven only by "black vengeance." He swears he will be constant in his revenge "by yond marble heaven."

O. Iago kneels beside Othello and swears to help Othello in his revenge, "what bloody work soever."

P. Othello accepts Iago's oath, and orders him to kill Cassio within three days.

Q. Iago pleads for Desdemona's life.

R. Othello says, "Damn her, lewd minx! O, damn her!" He tells Iago that he is going to "furnish me with some swift means of death / For the fair devil."

S. Othello appoints Iago his lieutenant, an office Iago accepts.

Once you have made your list of the incidents of the scene as a whole, re-read the section between Othello and Iago that ends Act III, Scene iii. Imagine questions that could arise when you consider the position of each act there in the string of acts that make up that scene in its entirety:

(Enter OTHELLO*)*

IAGO (CONTINUED)
                    Not poppy, nor mandragora,
Nor all the drowsy syrups of the world,
Shall ever medicine thee to that sweet sleep
Which thou ow'dst yesterday.

When Othello returns, Iago says he acts as if he were a changed man, a man incapable of "sweet sleep." Othello's entrance is placed after he has pushed aside the handkerchief and gone inside the citadel with Desdemona. He is returning from what is only the second time in the play when they, as husband and wife, have been alone together.

On stage, Emelia had picked up the handkerchief, used it to try to gain some sign of appreciation from her husband, and was rebuffed. Iago then announced his plan to plant the handkerchief in Cassio's lodgings.

Ask what specific behavior might Iago see that would prompt him to claim that Othello will never have another good night's sleep. To picture that act, keep speculating back in time. What previous act is positioned so that it might have stimulated Othello's visible behavior? Something Iago did? Could the fact that this incident is placed immediately after a private moment with Desdemona suggest that it might be something Desdemona did? Or something Othello himself did? Remember to choose a specific stimulating *event* (rather than a general state of mind), and see what that might suggest to you about the purposes at work at this moment.

OTHELLO
Ha! Ha! false to me?

IAGO
Why, how now, general? No more of that.

OTHELLO
Avaunt! be gone! Thou hast set me on the rack.
I swear 'tis better to be much abus'd
Than but to know't a little.

IAGO
                    How now, my lord?

OTHELLO

What sense had I of her stol'n hours of lust?
I saw't not, thought it not, it harm'd not me.
I slept the next night well, was free and merry;
I found not Cassio's kisses on her lips.
He that is robb'd, not wanting what is stol'n,
Let him not know't and he's not robb'd at all.

IAGO

I am sorry to hear this.

OTHELLO

I had been happy if the general camp,
Pioners and all, had tasted her sweet body,
So I had nothing known. O, now for ever
Farewell the tranquil mind! farewell content!
Farewell the plumed troops and the big wars
That make ambition virtue! O, farewell!
Farewell the neighing steed, and the shrill trump,
The spirit-stirring drum, th' ear-piercing fife,
The royal banner, and all quality,
Pride, pomp, and circumstance of glorious war!
And, O ye mortal engines, whose wide throats
Th' immortal Jove's great clamor counterfeit,
Farewell! Othello's occupation's gone!

In this passage, Othello describes the effects and costs of the loss of a tranquil mind. Once more, ask which specific previous event might be the trigger, the stimulus in Othello's mind, for this exchange.

The structure of the scene gives you a number to choose from. Could Othello be responding to the moment when Iago warned him against jealousy? Or might it be the moment when Iago noted that Othello's marriage to Desdemona is "unnatural?" What if it were Othello thinking of his earlier realization that his only "relief must be to loathe her"? Or could he be responding to the moment when he began to worry about Desdemona's "appetites," passions in her that he cannot control?

Once you have selected a particular "trigger" for this passage, ask, *given that choice*, what might Othello plausibly be trying to accomplish on stage as he says these words? If he is stimulated to speak by his memory of *that* particular incident, how might that memory logically lead him to try to make Iago do *this* particular thing right now?

Is he simply complaining? (Laurence Olivier and Anthony Quayle each have long experience and success in the role. Olivier quotes Quayle as saying, "The worst parts, the most difficult ones to bear, are the ones that are complaining all the time, the ones that moan . . . it's very tough on your imagination . . . Othello is all of that . . . ."[51])

Or might you imagine another Othello, one who is a character who initiates action rather than the traditional one who seems to be responding to Iago's manipulations? What if he were the one trying to persuade Iago of something? What? Might he be trying to prepare the ground for something he already intends to do? How could the position of Othello's attack on Iago ("Thou hast set me on the rack . . . ") support such a possibility?

IAGO

Is't possible, my lord?

OTHELLO

Villain, be sure thou prove my love a whore,
Be sure of it! Give me oracular proof:
Or by the worth of man's eternal soul,
Thou hadst been better have been born a dog
Than answer my wak'd wrath.

IAGO
                    Is't come to this?

OTHELLO

Make me see't; or, at the least, so prove it
That the probation bear no hinge nor loop
To hang a doubt on, or woe upon thy life!

IAGO

My noble lord,—

OTHELLO

If thou dost slander her and torture me,
Never pray more. Abandon all remorse;
On horror's head horrors accumulate;
Do deeds to make heaven weep, all earth amaz'd

For nothing canst thou to damnation add
Greater than that.

In this incident, Othello demands proof or he will kill Iago.

Ask, specifically, proof of what? Choose the particular crime uppermost in your Othello's mind. Given the position of this moment, what are the particular ways your Othello might understand the word "whore"?

That may not be as obvious a choice as traditional readings of the play would lead you to believe. One of the problems that has faced actors working on the role of Othello is the matter of the clock. The structure of incidents in the plot place Othello's wedding night just last night in the time scheme of the play, and it was interrupted, leaving Othello to spend most of the night quelling the civil disturbance Iago stirred up. In the days before the consummation of his marriage, Desdemona travelled to Cyprus in a boat with Emelia and Iago; Cassio and Othello each travelled on separate ships.

It's not unreasonable for you to ask, when was Desdemona supposed to have been unfaithful? Or, given the order of the incidents, in what particular sense of the word *could* she have been unfaithful? Or do you imagine an Othello who has forgotten how to keep track of time? What event might plausibly make the general of the Venetian military suddenly lose this competence? Olivier acknowledged this difficulty in his own preparation for the role:

> It is almost impossible to believe seriously that any human being on entirely uncorroborated evidence, as flimsy as a handkerchief embroidered with strawberries, could *that same night* strangle his wife in her bed and afterwards, in all sincerity, describe himself as " . . . one not easily jealous."[52]

At any rate, given the place in the plot where this demand occurs, why could your Othello choose this particular moment to ask for proof, and why might his immediate need be so great that he is willing to kill Iago if he hesitates to give him what he wants?

IAGO
                    O grace! O heaven defend me!
Are you a man? Have you soul or sense?
God be wi' you! Take mine office. O wretched fool!

That liv'st to make thine honesty a vice.
O monstrous world! Take note, take note, O world,
To be direct and honest is not safe.
I thank you for this profit, and from hence
I'll love no friend, sith love breeds such offense.

OTHELLO

Nay, stay. Thou shouldst be honest.

IAGO

I should be wise, for honesty's a fool,
And loses what it works for.

Iago's protest of injured honesty comes after a) he has hinted that Cassio's relationship with Desdemona is improper, b) he has taken his wife's gift of the handkerchief away from her in a peremptory and abusive manner, c) he has shared with the audience his thoughts about planting the handkerchief in Cassio's house, and d) Othello has threatened to kill him.

Imagine a pattern of behavior that connects these events with plausible consistency. Who is in control of this moment? Will you choose Iago, who finds a way of manipulating Othello's "honest" character to his own ends? What might those ends be? Or might it be Othello, the man who holds all the authority to kill here?

OTHELLO
By the world,
I think my wife be honest and think she is not;
I think that thou art just and think thou art not.
I'll have some proof. Her name, that was as fresh
As Dian's visage, is now begrim'd and black
As mine own face. If there be cords or knives,
Poison or fire or suffocating streams,
I'll not endure it. Would I were satisfied!

IAGO

I see, sir, you are eaten up with passion.
I do repent me that I put it to you.
You would be satisfied?

OTHELLO
Would? Nay, I will!

When Iago and Othello were alone before (Act III, Scene iii, 11. 92–276), Iago's appeal to trust and honesty evoked reasoned and reassuring answers from Othello. Now, in contrast, Iago says that Othello is "eaten up with passion." How might the progression of onstage events account for this change? Which specific event from the past will you choose as the spark that sets off this apparent fit of rage?

What you choose must have the effect of plausibly bringing about the next step, the step in which Iago asks what sort of evidence *will* satisfy Othello's immediate need for "proof":

IAGO
And may; but how? How satisfied, my lord?
Would you, the supervisor, grossly gape on,
Behold her topp'd?

OTHELLO
Death and damnation! O!

What might your Othello intend these general curses to mean? Which of the previous events indicated in the text is uppermost in his mind at this instant, do you suppose? Whom might he be threatening with death and damnation? Himself? Iago? The supposed lovers? The miserable dilemma in which he finds himself? Choose a specific focus for Othello's rage at this instant in the action.

Iago may or may not understand Othello's mind at this point; that choice is left to the imagination of the actor as well. What, specifically, might your Iago *think* he knows from Othello's outburst? Which previous incident might Iago believe is exploding in Othello's fevered thoughts?

And, if there is a difference between the two understood meanings behind Othello's response to Iago's suggestion that he "behold her topp'd," what specific and immediate conflict between the two characters might that suggest to you?

IAGO
It were a tedious difficulty, I think,
To bring them to that prospect. Damn them then,
If ever mortal eyes do see them bolster
More than their own. What then? how then?

What shall I say? Where's satisfaction?
It is impossible you should see this,
Were they as prime as goats, as hot as monkeys,
As salt as wolves in pride, and fools as gross
As ignorance made drunk. But yet, I say,
If imputation, and strong circumstances,
Which lead directly to the door of truth,
Will give you satisfaction, you may have't.

Iago suggests a substitute for direct proof; he lists the practical difficulties of catching the lovers *in flagrante,* but says that he can come up with circumstantial evidence if it "will give you satisfaction."

How might this step in the action be specifically shaped by the fact that it comes at a moment so soon after Iago has put the handkerchief in his pocket, saying he will use it to frame Cassio and Desdemona? How might your Iago prepare and lead up to this suggestion, knowing he has the prop he needs to stage this hoax? Will your Iago be one who improvises his villainy as he goes along, or one who has plans of action ready for implementation whenever the opportunity arises, or one who thinks fast when he suddenly discovers that he is faced with an enraged killer threatening him with death if he cannot come up with good proof? Other ideas?

OTHELLO
Give me a living reason she's disloyal.

What will your Othello mean when he accepts "living reason" as proof enough? What kind of proof will satisfy your Othello at this moment in the action? Is it the kind of proof that follows?

IAGO
I do not like the office;
But sith I am entered in this cause so far
(Prick'd to't by foolish honesty and love),
I will go on. I lay with Cassio lately;
And, being troubled with a raging tooth,
I could not sleep.
There are a kind of men so loose of soul
That in their sleeps will mutter their affairs.
One of this kind is Cassio.

In sleep I heard him say, 'Sweet Desdemona,
Let us be wary, let us hide our loves!'
And then, sir, would he gripe and wring my hand,
Cry out 'Sweet creature!' and then kiss me hard,
As if he pluck'd up kisses by the roots
That grew upon my lips, then laid his leg
Over my thigh, and sigh'd, and kiss'd, and then
Cried, 'Cursed fate, that gave thee to the Moor!'

OTHELLO

O monstrous! monstrous!

By any measure, this is an unlikely story. Lots of improvisations have been tried to justify this tale, suggesting Iago's homosexuality, Cassio's homosexuality (with scholarship demonstrating the idea that Florentine intellectuals were stereotypically presumed to be homosexuals), Othello's simple blindness to common sense at this extremity of his rage, and so on. You may find these promising speculations. But don't accept them until you have explored the difficulties posed by the placement this speech.

When, for example, was this encounter supposed to have happened? Again, Iago travelled to Cyprus, arriving yesterday with Desdemona and Emelia. Othello and Cassio were each in separate ships. Last night, Cassio and Iago were together carousing, but would Othello have imagined them in bed? It hardly seems likely. When Othello gets up (Do you suppose he ever returned to Desdemona's bed? The text suggests that Desdemona woke up alone, and that Othello was writing his letters to the Signory before dawn.) the next morning (*this* morning), he begins his day with a tour of the battlements and entrusting Iago with his official reports to the ministers back in Venice. Would he be likely to give such an important job to a man he suspected of sharing a bed last night with the man he has just cashiered for starting a civil upheaval in the streets?

So when is this "lately" that Iago has in mind? When did he have this toothache? Back in Venice? Is Iago likely to be sharing a bed with his superior officer, a stranger brought in from Florence to replace him in the chain of command? And sharing it while he is living with Emelia at home (no matter how neglectful a husband he may have been)? It is possible, but is it so obvious and persuasive a tale that Othello would accept this story as "proof" without asking a question? And yet he does.

So ask why your Othello might accept the story that reason and common sense (and the structure of the scene) make implausible. Could he be deliberately choosing to accept this unlikely gossip as the sort of evidence he needs? If so, how do you imagine this might make Othello behave as he accepts Iago's "monstrous" story? And how might that reaction impel Iago to offer a new understanding of the value of his story, one that, in the context of proofs to come, will give this circumstantial evidence the authority of literal proof?

IAGO
Nay, this was but his dream.

OTHELLO
But this denoted a foregone conclusion.

IAGO
'Tis a shrewd doubt, though it be but a dream;
And this may help to thicken other proofs
That do demonstrate thinly.

OTHELLO
I'll tear her all to pieces!

This is one of Othello's most violent, most threatening outbursts in the play. Why might it be placed at this moment? Could this be an involuntary reaction to the horror of Iago's news? Or might your Othello have an immediate purpose as he makes this threat? Might he be threatening Desdemona here? For whose benefit? Or could he be warning Iago? Or might another purposeful verb be at work? "Planning," or "informing," or "celebrating?" Try each one, and see what the implications are for the present, the past, and the future action of the play.

IAGO
Nay, but be wise. Yet we see nothing done;
She may be honest yet.

What reasons might impel Iago to counsel caution at this instant? How will your choice of immediate purpose for Iago be determined by the choice you just made for Othello's use of the outburst in the previous line; how might one plausibly follow the other?

And what response might Iago's hesitation provoke? Imagine a logic that makes this the moment to introduce the "evidence" of the handkerchief:

> IAGO
> Tell me but this:
> Have you not sometimes seen a handkerchief
> Spotted with strawberries in your wife's hand?
>
> OTHELLO
> I gave her such a one. 'Twas my first gift.
>
> IAGO
> I know not that; but such a handkerchief
> (I am sure it was your wife's) did I to-day
> See Cassio wipe his beard with.
>
> OTHELLO
> If it be that,—
>
> IAGO
> If it be that, or any that was hers,
> It speaks against her with the other proofs.

Speaking structurally, the striking thing about this handkerchief story is that only minutes before this assertion, within the same scene, Othello had that very handkerchief in his own hand. He specifically pushed it aside when Desdemona offered it to him.

One choice open to you, of course, is that he simply didn't notice, and that this headache exchange, even if it was understood to be rich with the imagery of cuckoldry, was a convenient device for the play-wright to get the handkerchief into the villain's hands. This is the traditional choice. But is it the only one?

Positioned as this incident is, with no break in time or place between the incident of the headache, the incident of Iago's capture of the handkerchief from Emelia, and this incident of presenting it as evidence, it's also possible that another Othello would find the story of the handkerchief as fantastical and impossible as the story of Cassio sharing a bed with Iago. Yet he could also find it promising as potentially useful "proof." Can you imagine an Othello who *needs* proof so much that he is willing to clutch at Iago's flimsy offerings of evidence even though, since he can tell time and he could reach judgments from his own experience, he knows that both pieces of evidence are patent lies? If you choose to imagine an Othello with his own agenda in this scene (*Why* does he need this proof so urgently?), might there also be an Iago who only provides Othello with the *means* for revenge rather than the cause? Think through the implications and possibilities of that sort of improvisation.

OTHELLO

O that the slave had forty thousand lives!
One is too poor, too weak, for my revenge.
Now do I see 'tis true. Look here, Iago;
All my fond love thus do I blow to heaven.

(Hisses contemptuously.)

'Tis gone.
Arise black vengeance, from thy hollow cell!
Yield up, O love, thy crown and hearted throne
To tyrannous hate. Swell, bosom, with thy fraught,
For 'tis of aspics' tongues!

IAGO

Pray, be content.

OTHELLO

O blood! Iago, blood!

IAGO

Patience, I say. Your mind, perhaps, may change.

Why might your Iago doubt Othello's resolve at this moment? Might feel he needs to test his own success? Could Iago be surprised to discover that Othello is so thoroughly and so quickly convinced? Might his skepticism be based on the fact that Othello's change of heart seems unnatural given the short time and the improvised evidence that appears to have brought it about?

At any rate, Othello's next speech, among his most famous passages, needs an immediate intention. What might Othello's objective be, once you notice that the "Like to the Pontic Sea" passage is placed as a response to Iago's suggestion that Othello might change his mind?

OTHELLO

Never Iago. Like to the Pontic sea,
Whose icy current and compulsive course
Ne'er feels retiring ebb, but keeps due on
To the Propontio and the Hellespont,
Even so my bloody thoughts, with violent pace,
Shall ne'er look back, ne'er ebb to humble love,
Till that a capable and wide revenge
Swallow them up.

Why might your Othello *need* to say these words at this moment?
Why could he need to convince Iago that he is going to carry out his
revenge no matter what? What might he expect Iago to do in response? Will your Iago do it? What visible event will make Othello
move on to the next step, the swearing of an oath?

(He kneels.)

Now, by yond marble heaven,
In the due reverence of a sacred vow
I here engage my words.

IAGO

Do not rise yet.

Iago makes a decision at this moment. Why do you suppose his
decision to join Othello in a vow happens at this point in the action?
Might he be trying to save his skin in the face of the torrent of rage
and murder he seems to have released? Or might he see his chance
to turn the general against his rival, Cassio? Or might he enjoy the
prospect of seducing Othello away from his wife, and having Othello
swear faith to him, Iago, instead? (More than one production has
compared this incident to a marriage.) Other ideas?

IAGO (CONTINUED)

Witness, you ever burning lights above!
You elements that clip us round about!
Witness that here Iago doth give up
The execution of his wit, hands, heart,

To wrong'd Othello's service! Let him command,
And to obey shall be in me remorse,
What bloody work soever.

(They rise.)

OTHELLO
                I greet thy love,
Not with vain thanks, but with acceptance bounteous,
And will upon the instant put thee to't.
Within these three days let me hear thee say
That Cassio's not alive.

Instantly, Othello asks for an assassination. What particular response will your Othello be trying to evoke as he issues this order right next to the vow?

Traditionally, Iago is in charge of the action here, controlling the course of events by stimulating Othello's passions in ways that suit Iago's purposes. Follow that logic through. What specific act on the part of Iago could have the visible effect of manipulating Othello into this quick command to kill?

Explore the possibilities of another improvisation of the scene, suggested by the proximity of the command to kill to the oath. Could it be Othello who is controlling the agenda here? Could he be the manipulator? What compelling act might Othello do at this moment that would have the visible effect of maneuvering Iago into accepting this criminal and dangerous assignment?

IAGO
My friend is dead; 'tis done as you request.
But let her live.

What event or response makes Iago choose this moment to plead for Desdemona's life? Will your Iago be asking for her salvation hypocritically, so as to maintain his disguise as an "honest" man? Can you imagine another Iago who discovers, at this moment, what Othello has had in mind all along, and tries to stop it? Perhaps a third Iago revels in the civil chaos that will probably follow when this black foreigner murders an innocent Venetian woman, and he makes this plea as a stimulus to Othello's rage?

OTHELLO
> Damn her, lewd minx! O, damn
her!
Come, go with me apart. I will withdraw
To furnish me with some swift means of death
For the fair devil.

Othello clearly rejects Iago's plea for Desdemona, at least to Iago. What might Othello mean to impart to Iago at this point in the action? For what purpose is he revealing a plan to murder her as well as one to murder Cassio?

Now imagine various ways Iago might understand what he is hearing: He is invited to follow Othello to a place where they can devise the way they will kill Desdemona, as if whether to kill were no longer a question. Does this put him in a position in which he might have to make a choice? What specific choices might you imagine Othello's invitation (or command) poses for Iago? Can you see him struggling to make up his mind? How might he choose? And why?

And when might he reach this decision?

OTHELLO   (Continued)
> Now art thou my lieutenant.

IAGO
I am your own for ever.

> *(Exeunt.)*

You've already noticed that there is a very short scene placed just before Act III, Scene iii. In it, Othello is on his way to inspect the battlements with some members of his staff. He has written various reports to be sent back to Venice. He hands these documents to Iago, and asks him to oversee their safe dispatch. Iago accepts this assignment.

At the time of the earlier incident, Cassio has already been cashiered. Iago is assuming Cassio's responsibilities. You might imagine that Iago, once Othello entrusts him with his official reports to the Signory of Venice, is now Othello's *de facto* lieutenant.

But this is the moment when Othello offers Iago the title. If your Iago shows that he agrees to help Othello kill Desdemona *before* the title is offered, that new title becomes Othello's reward for Iago's cooperation in a murder. If Iago agrees to join Othello *after* Othello called him his lieutenant, then the promotion acts as a bribe. Choose a place for Iago's decision. What kind of Iago, and what kind Othello might emerge from your choice of this order of events? Who will be in control?

Throughout your work with these scenes, the premise has been that the way actors and directors create an illusion for the stage is to imagine a new coherence for every element the script contributes to the final performance. Your work with the structure of a play—the design for the action laid out in the text—culminates that search. Every choice you have made, from the chain of physical action and reaction to the suggestions implicit in the playwright's manipulations of time, must be a logical suggestion for the coherence you are proposing for the stage. All of them need to enforce the particular connections you are making between the incidents as chosen and set in order by the playwright.

So, add up your choices for this scene. What consistent pattern of cause and effect, of stimulus and response is beginning to emerge as you explore the possible implications of the scene's structure? What are the consequences for the rest of the story you are beginning to discover?

Epilogue

My homework begins with reading the play—contriving an inno-cence if the play is familiar—setting my imagination free to react intuitively and simply to whatever the reading suggests. After a long rehearsal period, when the play has been so dismantled and probed that the simple elements, such as the story-line, or the bold outlines of a character or of a relationship, have become blurred or submerged with elaboration and detail, it is valuable to remind one-self of those first uncomplicated responses.[53]

—PATRICK STEWART

Patrick Stewart is offering good advice. All the bits of exciting im-provisation that may arise from a close reading of the text will mean very little in the theatre if the parts cannot be seen to add up to a whole, coherent play. You have been working on the scale of the scene, the single confrontation, the clear moment of crisis. The final job is to return to the source, the text as a whole.

Improvising a successful illusion for the whole play is based on the same principles as discovering your own sense of the parts, each step of each scene. The audience will find themselves willing to sus-pend their disbelief once they are brought to recognize that the broad events of the play are also plausible, likely, and persuasive. The en-gaging possibilities that inform each moment of the action must add up to a logic that is able to inform the complete play. This is why Patrick Stewart returns, at the end, to remind himself of a fundamental story, a broad sketch of his character, the first impressions that struck him as he began to read.

The return to the broad strokes of the text suggests a sort of pyramidal scheme at work. Each step is completed in your imagination as you consider the effects on action suggested by the circumstances; fictional intentions; moments of discovery and decision; and the craft of the playwright in shaping language, time, and structure. Once each step is complete, these immediate steps are assembled into larger blocks of action on the scale of the scene, blocks that come to have a clear significance when you take those same factors into account. And these scenes, in turn, will add up to an overriding struggle, a defining problem for the characters to resolve, a unifying pursuit that is the action of the play as a whole. It's that unifying pursuit that caps off the pyramid.

Consider an entire text in the light of the broadest circumstances and intentions at work in the play. What you'll find, of course, is that even the unifying pursuit that defines the action is open to improvisation. You may assemble the many pieces of improvised action you've discovered and choose to imagine a *Hamlet* that is primarily about the action of trying to restore the throne of Denmark to its rightful succession. But you may also choose to imagine another *Hamlet*, describing its action as the prince trying to win back the love and faith of Gertrude, or as Hamlet testing Claudius's court to find an effective way to achieve the revenge of his father's command. Your *Romeo and Juliet* may emphasize a story about young people struggling with the perils of their own sexual awakening, or it may be about a series of attempts to resolve a pointless civil war. Your *Othello* may reveal the tale of manipulating a gullible husband to murder, or perhaps another story about a gifted black man fighting back against the white Venetians who have so disillusioned him. You choose.

The point is that for the text as a whole, as for each moment of each scene, the search is for an action, for an active verb that can serve as the determining element for the spectacle to come. To reach a theatrical understanding of these texts, you read on until you have imagined the most promising fictional pursuit to define the story and complete its illusion.

Robertson Davies, the actor, playwright, and novelist, has one of his characters say:

> ... When I say imagination, I mean the capacity to see all sides of a subject and weigh all possibilities; I don't mean fantasy and ... moonshine; Imagination is a good horse to carry you over the ground, not a flying carpet to set you free from probability.[54]

This, too, is good advice. Improvising Shakespeare requires a good horse to carry you over the ground, a firm sense of what is probable. It is *after* you have established these imaginative probabilities that you, and your audience, may get a ride on a flying carpet.

Recommended Readings

Theory:

ARISTOTLE: *The Poetics*, S.H. Butcher (trans.), Hill and Wang, New York, 1961.
BALL D: *Backwards and Forwards*, Southern Illinois University Press, Carbondale, 1983.
BROOK P: *The Empty Space*, Avon Books, New York, 1968.
———— *The Shifting Point: 1946–1987*, Harper & Row, New York, 1987.
———— *The Open Door*, Pantheon Books, New York, 1993.
BRUDER M, COHN LM *et al.: A Practical Handbook for the Actor*, Vintage Books, New York, 1986.
GOODWIN J (Ed.): *The Royal Shakespeare Theatre Company, 1960–63*, Theatre Arts Books, New York, 1964.
GIELGUD J: *Stage Directions*, Random House, New York, 1963.
GUTHRIE T: *A Life in the Theatre*, McGraw-Hill, New York, 1959.
LANGER S: *Feeling and Form*, Chas. Scribner & Sons, New York, 1953.
NAGLER AM: *A Sourcebook in Theatrical History*, Dover, New York, 1952.
SONTAG S: *Against Interpretation*, Anchor Books, New York, 1966.
STANISLAVSKI C: *An Actor Prepares*, Elizabeth Reynolds Hopgood (trans.), Theatre Arts Books, New York, 1948.
TURNER F: *Natural Classicism*, Paragon House, New York, 1985.

Practice:

BARTON J: *Playing Shakespeare*, Methuen, London, 1984.
BERRY R: *On Directing Shakespeare*, Hamish Hamilton, London, 1989.

BROCKBANK P: *Players of Shakespeare 1*, Cambridge University Press, Cambridge, England, 1985.

BROWN JR (Ed.): *Shakespeare in Performance: An Introduction Through Six Major Plays*, Harcourt Brace Jovanovich, New York, 1976.

BURTON (Ed.): *Great Acting*, BBC, London, 1967.

COLE T, AND CHINOY HK: *Directors on Directing*, Bobbs-Merril Company, New York, 1963.

GOODWIN J (Ed.), *Peter Hall's Diaries*, Hamish Hamilton, London, 1983.

HAGEN U: *Respect for Acting*, MacMillan, New York, 1973.

JACKSON R, SMALLWOOD R (Eds.): *Players of Shakespeare 2*, Cambridge University Press, Cambridge, England, 1988.

————: *Players of Shakespeare 3*, Cambridge University Press, Cambridge, 1993.

OLIVIER L: *Confessions of an Actor*, Simon and Schuster, New York, 1982.

————: *On Acting*, Simon and Schuster, New York, 1986.

REDFIELD W: *Letters from an Actor*, Viking Press, New York, 1967.

SELBOURNE D: *The Making of a Midsummer Night's Dream*, Methuen, London, 1982.

SHAKESPEARE W: *The Complete Works*, Cambridge Edition Text, Garden City Books, New York, 1936.

SHER A: *Year of the King*, Limelight Editions, New York, 1985.

Notes

1. Peter Brook, *The Open Door*, Pantheon Books, New York, 1993, p. 113.
2. Russell Jackson, and Robert Smallwood (Eds.), *Players of Shakespeare 3*, Cambridge University Press, Cambridge, England, 1993, p. 191.
3. Peter Brook, *op. cit.*, p. 102.
4. Suzanne Langer, *Feeling and Form*, Chas. Scribner's Sons, New York, 1953. Ch. 17, "The Dramatic Illusion."
5. Alfred Harbage, *William Shakespeare: A Reader's Guide*, Noonday Press, New York, 1963, pp. 319–320.
6. William Redfield, *Letters from an Actor*, Viking Press, New York, 1967, pp. 113–115.
7. Alfred Harbage, *op. cit.* p. 3.
8. Frederick Turner, *Natural Classicism*, Paragon House, New York, 1985, p. 237.
9. John Barton, *Playing Shakespeare*, Methuen, London, 1984, p. 2.
10. Russell Jackson and Robert Smallwood (Eds.), *Players of Shakespeare 2*, Cambridge University Press, Cambridge, England, 1988.
11. Barrett H. Clark, *European Theories of the Drama*, Henry Popkin, (Ed.), Crown Publishers, New York, 1965, p. 416.
12. Aristotle, *The Poetics*, Ch. 9.
13. David Selbourne, *The Making of a Midsummer Night's Dream*, Methuen, London, 1982, p. 45.
14. John Barton, *op. cit.* p. 50.
15. Suzanne Langer, *op. cit.*
16. For a detailed discussion of this technique, see David Ball, *Backwards and Forwards*, Southern Illinois University Press, Carbondale, 1983.

17. Ralph Berry, *On Directing Shakespeare,* Hamish Hamilton, London, 1989, pp. 27–28.
18. Hal Burton (Ed.), *Great Acting,* BBC, London, 1967 p. 22.
19. John Goodwin (Ed.), *Peter Hall's Diaries,* Hamish Hamilton, London, 1983, p. 188.
20. Uta Hagen, *Respect for Acting,* Macmillan, New York, 1973, p. 186.
21. David Mamet, "He's the Kind of Guy Who . . . ", *Theatre Week,* Jan. 22, 1990.
22. Hal Burton, *op. cit.,* p. 96.
23. William Redfield, *op. cit.,* p. 194.
24. Ralph Berry, *op. cit.,* p. 115.
25. Russell Jackson and Robert Smallwood, *Players of Shakespeare 2.* pp. 139–140.
26. John Goodwin (Ed.), *op. cit.,* p. 188.
27. John Barton, *op. cit.,* p. 12.
28. *Ibid.,* p. 82.
29. Laurence Olivier, *On Acting,* Weidenfield and Nicholson, London, 1986, pp. 116–118.
30. Antony Sher, *Year of the King,* Limelight Editions, New York, 1992, pp. 18, 158.
31. Gerard Raymond, "Sir Ian McKellen's *Richard III,*" *Theatre Week,* June 15, 1992, p. 14.
32. Julie Hankey (Ed.), *Plays in Performance: Richard III,* Junction Books, London, 1981, p. 69.
33. Antony Sher, *op. cit.* p. 187.
34. Julie Hankey, *op. cit.,* p. 70.
35. *Ibid,* p. 106.
36. Russell Jackson and Robert Smallwood (Eds.), *Players of Shakespeare 2,* p. 83.
37. Peter Brook, "*Shakespearean Realism,*" *The Shifting Point: 1946–1987,* Harper & Row, New York, 1987, pp. 84–85.
38. John Goodwin (Ed.), *op. cit.* p. 180.
39. Constantin Stanislavski, *An Actor Prepares,* Elizabeth Reynolds Hapgood (trans.), Theatre Arts Books, New York, 1948, p. 186.
40. John Barton, *op. cit.,* p. 94.
41. *Ibid,* p. 132.
42. *Ibid,* p. 160.
43. Philip Brockbank, *Players of Shakespeare 1,* Cambridge University Press, London, 1985, p. 50.
44. John Russell Brown (Ed.), *Shakespeare in Performance: An Introduction Through Six Major Plays,* Harcourt Brace Jovanovich, New York, 1976, p. 235.
45. *Ibid,* p. 236.

46. *Ibid.*
47. *Ibid*, p. 237.
48. Philip Brockbank, *op. cit.*, pp. 50–51.
49. John Russell Brown, *op. cit.*, pp. 238–239.
50. Russell Jackson and Robert Smallwood (Eds.), *Players of Shakespeare 3*, p. 122.
51. Hal Burton (Ed.), *op. cit.*, p. 26.
52. Laurence Olivier, *Confessions of an Actor*, Simon and Schuster, New York, 1982, p. 253.
53. Philip Brockbank, *op. cit.*, p. 14.
54. Robertson Davies, *The Deptford Trilogy*, Penguin Books, London, 1977, p. 475.

Index